This. This. This. Is. Love. Love. Love.
Stories

This. This. This. Is. Love. Love. Love.
Stories

Jennifer Wortman

Split Lip Press

Published by Split Lip Press
333 Sinkler Road
Wyncote, PA 19095
www.splitlippress.com

ISBN: 9781070561516

Cover Art by Jayme Cawthern

For John

Table of Contents

Love You. Bye.

My psychic friend sees light cords extending between people and their phones. But, she says, unlike the glowing metaphysical threads of relationship that stretch between two sentient beings, these cords don't attach at both sides. They end abruptly at the phone, terminating in a right angle that slips frantically against the chem-armored plastic. This dynamic, she contends, explains our depression epidemic: the great unrequited love in late capitalism between people and their things. An unattached light cord, like a chest of drawers moved alone, weighs down its carrier, is almost impossible to bear. I think of this as I, a longtime depressive, stand in line in a glaring white store at a cacophonous mall to purchase my first smart phone. It's 2016 and I'm so behind that I no longer take pride in my small, pointless gesture against technocracy, all the more pointless because of my addiction to every other screen in my life. In 2016, I'm embarrassed. I'm ashamed.

My psychic friend's powers are useless to her. So she tells me as I sit on the floor of her studio apartment, gazing up at her as she perches on the edge of her unmade bed with her latest complaints. She's been down lately. Has she lost weight? I ask if she's eaten. She's not hungry, she says.

"Maybe a small snack? Dry Cheerios?"

She looks at me funny. "I'll eat later."

But I know where these complaints, this appetite loss, can lead, from my own days of dry Cheerios. At a crisis-hotline operator's bidding, I'd crawled to my kitchen to retrieve them, doing my best, as I moved, to sustain the feeling of hiding in bed. I say "crawled," but really I lurched, launching forward then resting on the gritty floor, all the while keeping the phone to my ear for coaching from my new best friend. That phone had a cord that I stretched, but not far: my apartment then was small, shrinking by the day.

My turn at the new-phone counter, a black snake in the middle of the room. My heart thumps triply hard, stirred by the triple threat of a business transaction with a stranger in a shopping mall. The phone boy, like all the phone boys, is young, wily, and thin, a touch of cool in his short hair, his company-logo polo, white as the walls, strapped into his business-cas pants. I wave my prehistoric phone at him, a practical unnecessity but a spiritual must. He is my confessor and my phone is my confession. Forgive me. I don't belong in this world.

Most people, bemoans my friend, don't want to hear about their light cords. Much worse than them are the people who do. They want to know everything: color, texture, intensity, diameter, circumference, penumbra, odor, taste. They want to know more. They call in the middle of the night, asking questions she can't answer. She knows light cords and that's all.

A light cord can express something about a relationship in its present form. It doesn't tell the future or explain the past. Although the past and future might be inferred from the condition of the light cord, and is, in fact, almost always obvious and predictable, the obviousness and predictability come from the tedium of human behavior rather than the cords themselves. And the word "almost" is key. Sometimes my friend's inferences are wrong. When she was young, she preferred to advise rather than predict. But those who craved her advice most, those late-night callers with insatiable needs, were the least likely to take it. So now she neither advises nor predicts, except for the occasional grim prediction, about others, to me.

She agrees to go for a walk: a good sign. We pass a couple whose light cord is bright black, dim purple, dried-blood brown, the tendrils knotted and thick, some plunged into the woman's chest, some wound around her neck. Abusive relationships, my friend tells me, have the strongest cords. That woman will never leave him. But sometimes they do, I say. Sometimes they leave. You have no idea, says my friend. You don't see what I see. The odds are infinitesimal. But it could happen, I say. By your own admission, you never know. She stares at me, her dark eyes darkening. I'm her longtime depressive friend. Why am I on the side of hope?

"It could happen," she says. "But it won't."

———

Unsurprisingly, the phone boy laughs at my phone. Or maybe he's just laughing at me, at my overreactive face, which I'm sure now conveys an excess of shame and fear. But it's a kind laugh, and I fall for him a bit. Then he says, "Yeah, I don't want to join this century either. But you gotta do what you gotta do, right?"

"Right." I sigh, adding extra wind and a shoulder collapse for his benefit. He laughs again and I smile. He's one of those clean-cut blonds with electric blue eyes I don't consider my type until they aim those eyes at me.

Things turn serious: We talk phones. We talk plans. Radiating confidence and concern, he gives me choices, explains pros and cons. He helps me find the best phone and plan for me.

By the time I leave the store, I am in love.

I persuade my friend to see a therapist, one I've researched and vetted, though not my own. I've spoken at length to my therapist about my psychic friend. I'd love nothing more than for my therapist to treat us both, a sort of psychological *ménage à trois* that would certainly bring us all closer in a perverse and risky way. But, for that very reason, along with my attraction to that reason, my therapist says no.

Now that we're in the car, my friend, who has agreed to go to the therapist, doesn't want to go to the therapist. She regales me with tales of a therapist she had in high school, when her parents made her go because they'd learned about the light cords. He was condescending, she says. And dense. She despised him, despite the fact that he reassured her parents that she was absolutely fine. Maybe that's why she despised him. The only therapist she's ever had. "A good therapist is hard to find," I say, trying to sympathize. "But—"

"You know what?" she interrupts. "I hope we get lost and crash the car and The Misfit comes along and shoots us in the chest."

I'm at a coffee place, ordering chamomile tea, the closest thing they have to the opposite of coffee. My nervous system can't handle caffeine. I sit down. I've brought work, a laptop with a manuscript I'm copyediting. This is one of those painfully engineered coffee spots where a table is never just a table: this table contains chalkboards. Normally, before I start work, I take a few minutes to color: "making shapes" my boyfriend calls it. If a writing utensil should come into my hand, be it near a chalkboard or margin or scrap, I'll scribble until a thick curve emerges. From there, offshoots: more curves, and negative space trapped within, until I've created something that looks nothing like a person but somehow evokes a human, uniquely graceful and deformed. This soothes me. But today, I don't color. As soon as I sit down, I take out my phone. Yes, my laptop could fill the same function, but it takes time to load, whereas my new phone offers itself up to me quick. How can I refuse such kindness? How can I reject holding such bounty close, in just one little hand?

"Ha!" someone says. It's such a gleefully accusing "ha" that I instantly know it's directed at me. The phone boy. "I knew it! You're just like the rest of us."

He wears an untucked t-shirt that hugs his leanness, and without his work uniform, without his paycheck hanging overhead, he beams a beautiful insanity, his bright blue eyes now neon, his cropped blond hair electric.

"I never said I wasn't," I reply, though he's onto something, the way I fetishize my alienation. I'm only a little piqued—I like a man who's onto something.

"Your old phone said it all." He winks.

"I can't be the only one who comes in with old phones."

"Oh, you're not. But they've usually got a few decades on you." He flips a chair around and straddles it, folding his arms atop the back, a posture engaged yet detached, temporary. I'm pretty sure I've got a decade on him, and I can't believe he's landed beside me for even a small moment, let alone remembered me.

In my joyous bewilderment, I toss out a joke. "The only thing this phone's missing is a needle, so I can shoot it straight into my veins."

"Ha!" He slaps the top of the chair. "Love it."

My psychic friend tells me that her new therapist views her anger as a good sign. The therapist believes she's not clinically depressed. Most depressed women, her therapist says, turn their anger inward, and that's when things go seriously south. I suspect her therapist is in love with her, as are most people.

My psychic friend is beautiful, with her long black hair and deep amber eyes, the play of light and dark within. But what people most love about her is more felt than observed, a power she emanates and, in good times, shares. Their experiences with her are all about their overwhelming experience of her, as if she were but a memorable dream, theirs alone. The proof: hardened skeptics accept her psychic abilities without question. Others aren't psychic, they think, but the usual boring rules don't apply to her.

I ask her to read the light cord between me and my boyfriend. She says no. I ask her to read the light cord between me and her. She says no fucking way. She's taken the day off work. She's told her boss at the boutique where she sells, without trying, tons of long, flowing skirts to women who want to look like her, that she's sick, which I believe isn't a lie.

"Can I get you anything?" I ask.

"Why do you want me to be depressed?" she asks.

"Why would I want you to be depressed?"

"I don't know," she says. "You tell me."

The phone boy, of course, is in a band: lead vocals and rhythm guitar. He's at the coffee place, I learn, to firm up an acoustic gig, which he invites me to in a casually-promoting-his-band sort of way. Still, the invitation so excites me that once he leaves, I can't work. I find myself rereading sentences, my elation brightening the space between each word until the manuscript becomes that bright space, its words incidental. I shut the computer and go home. A good run is in order. Instead, I call my boyfriend and invite him to the phone boy's show.

"I can't. I've got a late home-visit that night." My boyfriend is a guardian *ad litem*, a lawyer who represents the interests of abused and neglected children. Part of his job involves visiting kids' homes.

Though I ask and ask, he won't tell me what he sometimes finds. This is one of the reasons I love him. At home, at all hours, he takes work calls in both English and Spanish, and either way I understand just enough to know I understand nothing. Though I ask and ask, he won't tell me what he's discussed. This is another reason I love him. In fact, I love him so much that he's not just my boyfriend. He's my fiancé—though I have a hard time calling him that, for fear of cursing us both.

What he does tell me about his job: It's important, when possible, to keep families together. But sometimes it's not possible.

I genuinely want him to come with me to the phone boy's show. Not just because I love him, but to protect that love from the new excitement taking over my brain. Deep down, though, I also crave the charge of having him and the phone boy in the same room. I am a terrible person, and worse still because though I genuinely want him to come to the phone boy's show, I'm also genuinely thrilled he can't.

"Love you," I say. "Bye."

Years ago, when I'd called the crisis hotline about my depression, the operator asked if I'd ever been hospitalized. I dropped my Cheerios box. "Are you going to hospitalize me?" I screeched. This was one of my lifelong fears, that I'd end up locked in a hospital because I couldn't get my shit together. Sometimes I fantasized about it, that life would be easier there, my every move choreographed and assessed for its fitness, my weaknesses laid bare and swept up by routine. But this fantasy of escape belied its own trap: if I landed in a hospital, I would always be in that hospital, even when I got out. I imagined it as a marriage, that other institution, a public "I do" to my depression. Depression and I had dated off and on for years. And sometimes depression fucked me good. But I didn't want to marry it, and the day I called that hotline, my depression seemed a final fate: an arranged marriage I lacked the strength to defy.

I was sick, alright. The twin tents of my hipbones, the siren song of kitchen blades, the mounds of trash I couldn't take out because I feared going outside. The teaching job I loved that I soon would lose, because I'd not only lost the ability to function—I'd lost the will. Now I'd be taken away, as I should.

Still: "I don't want to go to the hospital," I cried into the phone. "Please."

"You're not going to the hospital," the hotline guy said. "I promise. It's just a routine question for our records. You're okay. You're okay." He sounded not okay. "I'm sorry. I'm new at this. I handled that wrong."

It was his distress, my concern for him, that had finally calmed me down.

"I care about other people," I want to tell my psychic friend. "Not just myself. I want you to be happy. I want you to be nice." But already, I've undermined my own argument. So I tell her nothing and just look at her hard, so she can see the hurt on my face before she turns toward the wall.

I grab my phone, find Facebook, and search for the phone boy.

It takes all my willpower not to ask my boyfriend what I should do about my love for the phone boy. In fact, my willpower fails and I find ways to ask him in flimsy code.

"What do you do with overwhelming feelings that you don't want to have?"

"I shout in my car during my commute."

"Do you shout about me?"

"Of course not."

"What do you do with overwhelming feelings that you kind of want to have?"

He shrugs. "I act on them if I can." This is true. He has overwhelming feelings for marijuana, so he smokes marijuana. He has overwhelming feelings for computer chess, so he plays computer chess. He has overwhelming feelings for soccer, so he plays soccer. He has overwhelming feelings for me, so he's marrying me. When he's with me, he's with me, but when he's with marijuana, or chess, or soccer, I'm gone. That's another thing I love about him: his complete devotion to whatever's before him.

"What if you can't act on them?" I ask.

He looks at me with a sweet tilt of his head. Like water, his eyes are blue, grey, or green depending on the light, and I want to swim there. The growing lines around his eyes are somehow boyish: a child's drawing of sun beams. Because he looks younger than he is, he wears a beard, dark brown against his copper skin, and sometimes I want to live there, a flea in a warm forest.

"What's going on?" he asks.

"Nothing," I say, but my face seizes like an animal caught.

———

I "like" the phone boy's band on Facebook and check the page constantly. What do I think I will find there? I don't know, but that doesn't stop me from searching his face every few seconds. Love, perhaps, is the opposite of depression. It pulls me into the world. If it pulls me too hard, all the better; the opposing forces in me are strong. And, yes, I'm aware that this pulling, this bumpy trajectory of drag, bounce, and burn might not be love at all, but something else: the need to be pulled. But toward what? The phone boy's pretty face is oblivious to the churning questions it raises. He stares off to the side with a fetching lack of smile, his eyes gleaming with secret knowledge: who he is, what he thinks, what he wants. The sacred mysteries. If I stare long enough, maybe that face will tell me what it knows. If I stare long enough, maybe I can tell it what I know too. When I tell him, will he look away?

My boyfriend doesn't look away. It's a beautiful thing. Why isn't it enough? Why this hole in me as big as the Internet?

After much persuasion, my psychic friend comes with me to the phone boy's show. Her hair is matted, her clothes, wrinkled. Still, when she enters the coffee shop, people turn toward her.

I don't tell her how I feel about the phone boy. I'm sure she can see the light cords radiating across the coffee place. Maybe my cords rub up against him, unwelcome, like they rub against my new phone. Maybe his cords stretch elsewhere. Maybe, as soon as he lays eyes on my psychic friend, his cords will reach inside her and make her his.

In the past, my psychic friend would tell me whatever I wanted to know about light cords, my own and others. In fact, I was one of those people who wanted to know everything, who called her with questions at night. Nothing she told me was enough. If she gave me a color, I wanted the shade. If she gave me the shade, I wanted the meaning of the shade. If she gave me the meaning of the shade, I'd want a better, clearer meaning of the shade, a meaning that didn't exist. My psychic friend no longer tells me about my light cords. When she first started refusing me, we'd both laugh. Her laughter acknowledged my neuroses with a protective affection. My laughter understood, and appreciated, her protection. But over time, as I continued to press her for light-cord intel, the laughter stopped.

When I tire of the endless, unanswerable questions inspired by the phone boy's Facebook picture, I find my show on Netflix, which reduces my constant questions to one urgent query: "What happens next?" In my own life, that question is attended by myriad anxieties and grim hypotheticals. When I watch my show, though, the question of what happens next neutralizes. I disappear.

My boyfriend and I like and dislike the same high-brow shows: yes to the bloody medieval fantasy epic, no to Gidget goes to prison; yes to 60s ad men, no to the political drama with the cheesy fourth-wall breaks. When others ask us if we watch Gidget goes to prison, a current passes between us: one of us will say, "No," and leave it at that, but we will silently savor the memory of discussing why Gidget goes to prison is a bad show. We will savor the common values that led us to dislike the show.

If our shared show affirms our connection, our separate shows affirm our independence. We like to affirm our independence, yet we are sheepish with each other about our separate shows, whose flagrant inferiority we cleave to like pillows at the end of a hard day. Our separate shows, we understand, are nowhere near as good as our shared shows, which we share because they transcend the parting in our tastes. For our separate shows, he likes the post-apocalypse, I like teen dramas. He likes superheroes, I like lovelorn doctors. Sometimes one of us will walk past the other's show and laugh at what's on the screen. More often, though, we repress our laughs: a small kindness. The sort of kindness I fear, in time, goes away.

The coffee house at night has an upscale log cabin ambiance: ceiling lights brighten ubiquitous wood. We find seats, at a round table with others, a couple of my psychic friend's admirers who motion us over, make room for us in the crowd. Our benefactors are a couple, aging hippies: the man has a red, happy face and long cottony hair; the woman is plump-cheeked and seems amazed by everything her eyes take in. Before we turn our chairs toward the stage, a strange, sad look passes across my psychic friend's face.

"That couple," she whispers, "they're perfect together."

"What do their cords look like?"

She puts her finger to her mouth and shakes her head. "Not now."

But I have to ask. "Do they look like my cords with Felipe?"

"If you have to ask, you know the answer," she hisses.

"Bullshit! People ask things because they don't know the answer!" I've gotten too loud in a loud room. A couple people break from the sea of voices to eyeball me, and I smile apologetically, a small, sad folding-in of my lips. The band, sans phone boy, is onstage, fiddling with equipment.

"The show's starting," my psychic friend says, even though it isn't.

I sip at my tea before it cools and enjoy the burn.

When I was in high school, I dated a boy. I drank a lot back then, and once, at a party my then-boyfriend didn't attend, I kissed another boy. I told my boyfriend and begged his forgiveness. A few months later, he told me he'd slept with my friend and broke up with me for her.

When I was in college, I dated a boy. I drank a lot back then, and once, at a party my then boyfriend didn't attend, I kissed another boy. I told my boyfriend and begged his forgiveness. A few weeks later, he told me he'd slept with his housemate and broke up with me for her.

When I was in my twenties, I dated a man. I drank a lot back then. Enough said.

All I think about these days is kissing the phone boy. I try not to think about it. No, that's a lie. I relish thinking about it. That first touch of lips—and from that softness springs violence, the push to consume, a reminder of teeth, cruel boundaries of flesh.

If I kiss the phone boy, there's no question: I know what happens next.

———

The phone boy arrives and takes his place on stage. I search the band for signs of anger at his lateness, but everyone's calm. The phone boy narrows in on his guitar, which he plugs, plucks, and strums with facility and care. He straps it over himself; it hangs from him half-uniform, half-weapon, and he smiles broadly at no one—with just a small hint of evil I feel in my gut—and checks the mike. I catch his eye, and the little nod he gives me makes me beam like a moron.

"Why isn't Felipe here?" my psychic friend asks. I don't like how her voice slows with his name, as if milking its sweetness.

"He's at work. A home-visit for a really rough case," I say, trying to change the subject while racking up virtue by association. "He won't tell me the details."

She nods at the stage. "You're engaged, for Christ's sake. And, trust me, blondie up there's not into you."

"Hey, everyone," says the phone boy. "We're The Nut Jobs." His hand crashes against the guitar and they're off. "I think it's time for me to find another basement," he sings. "'Cause I can hardly stand the feeling I get when I'm in your shoes."

My psychic friend stares at me while I stare at the phone boy. I'm stuck. If I look away, she'll see it as a concession. If my eyes stay put, she'll take that as proof. What did I think would happen? She'd chuckle at my reaching light cords and say, "Poor thing! Let's talk"? Once, she would have done just that. But those days are gone.

Tears fill my eyes, but I grin like a moron again and let the two of us stare where we will.

———

When I first met my psychic friend, she had a way of looking at me that made me feel seen. I was buying the long, flowing skirt I'd hoped would make me become her and she smiled with such warmth that I instantly just wanted to be myself. On a whim, I invited her to my open mike performance that night, my first since my bad depression. I'd invited no one else. I was afraid I couldn't go through with it. Even in the best of times, performing got me puking pre-show.

A pretentious friend once said to me, "For artists, friends are like lovers, and lovers are like gods." But he wasn't wrong. I'm no longer an artist of any sort. Music was too painfully public and writing, which I took up next, too painfully private. Art had always seemed like a natural offshoot of my mood disorders, even a justification for them. If I could make great art, then my stupid suffering would mean something. But anxiety made it hard for me to sing. And depression made it impossible for me to write. Nothing's worse for despair than the blank page: the power it seemingly grants and ultimately withholds. Some say depression rises from helplessness; might it rise, instead, from a fear of power?

My psychic friend came to the open mike and sat with me as I trembled. Here's the thing: when I got on stage, the fright disappeared. The music pumping through me, I became someone else, someone who made people stop sipping and chatting and scanning the room. On a good night, the air went electric: I turned both source and surge.

My psychic friend came on a good night.

"I want to be your second dog," I sang.

I always left the stage gutted and stunned; what I'd unleashed boomeranged with the force of a slap. If, for a moment, I'd thought I was everything, I must surely be nothing.

"That was beautiful," my psychic friend said, and I believed her, though I never believed such compliments.

"Thank you," I said to my new friend. "That means a lot."

The phone boy, despite his job, makes only rudimentary use of technology. The Nut Jobs' Facebook page is minimal: no music samples. And the music itself is plugged in for volume only, asserting its low-fi sound all the more. The instruments—guitar, drums, bass—supply stacks of rhythm. The phone boy's baritone dips inside the music: it digs, it damns.

"Hey there, you're looking fine," he sings, "I'll erase your history if you'll rewrite mine." I believe.

His phrasings bend with a bit of blues, then sting with a touch of twang. Any irony is drenched in feeling. Any feeling is cut with gristle. Even my psychic friend watches him intently now, her features pressed between rage and awe.

"He's really good," she says.

"I know." Though I hadn't known, or even cared, at all, until now.

At the set break, I'm afraid to approach him for even some quick praise. But if I don't approach him, why am I here? If I do approach him, why am I engaged to my boyfriend? Why, at this moment, do I believe my engagement doesn't exist? When you leave the kitchen, does the table within still exist? Common sense says of course. Philosophy deliberates. The animal says, where's the food in the room I'm in now?

I stand. I walk forward. Beside me, my psychic friend stands and walks too.

My boyfriend says he will never cheat on me. Cheaters disgust him. His father cheated on his mother. His ex-girlfriend cheated on him. When someone cheats in a movie, he turns from the screen and groans. Therefore, I've long expected he will cheat on me, just as the fire-and-brimstone televangelist will inevitably reveal himself as a pedophile.

At the same time, I believe him. Believing allows me to distinguish him: This relationship is different. He's the man who will never cheat on me. He, and therefore we, are exceptional. But even though I believe he won't cheat on me, I hold onto my simultaneous disbelief like a sick hope. If he's the man who will one day cheat on me despite his best efforts and deeply held values, then I am the woman who may behave with impunity.

A secret about my boyfriend, who is universally admired as a sweet, gentle man: he often imagines slitting people's throats. Not only does he imagine it, but he plans it down to the detail: the wheres, whens, hows. This secret, and the fact that only I know about it, is yet another reason I love him. He says, "I have a lot of impulses I control every day. I can be attracted to someone else without wanting to act on it."

"Are you attracted to someone else?"

"That's not the point."

"It's exactly the point." I ask him if he's attracted to my psychic friend.

"What?" he says, flamboyantly dumbfounded, as if I'd just

suggested he was attracted to a pile of poop. "No!"

This is when I realize that despite being distinguished in so many ways, my boyfriend, like everyone else, wants to fuck my psychic friend.

When we get to the phone boy, my psychic friend turns shy, clasping her hands and bowing her head like a penitent. What fun she and I could have had, in better times, making and dodging eye contact, trying not to laugh. The phone boy's talking to someone else, a tall, mustachioed dude who draws the phone boy's gaze up and away. The phone boy nods, laughs, slaps the guy's shoulder, all with a showman's ease that cloaks the rawness we saw on stage. I want to kill him for that ease. I also want to stick my tongue down his throat. I prepare to make my attention-grab, a playful poke to the back, but before I do anything, he whirls around, as if spun by rope.

"Hey!" he says. "It's the phone girl."

The synchronicity bowls me over. I almost confess everything, tell him he's my phone boy and take him out back. But then it occurs to me he might have forgotten my name. "Aren't we all phone girls?" I say. "At your store?"

"You're a feisty one," he says. "I like it. You having fun?"

Fun—abused, overused word—doesn't cut it. After childhood, nothing is fun. Pleasures are always complicated by pains—or derive from them. Still, I open my mouth to cry, "Yes!" But my psychic friend beats me to it.

"I could listen to you all night," she says softly, or rather, in a forceful voice that feigns softness, its edges fluffed.

I expect him to lob back a flirtatious quip. What he says instead, the showman draining from his face, is worse: "Thank you. That means a lot."

My engagement ring doesn't fit my ring finger. It's an heirloom passed down from my boyfriend's Colombian great-grandmother, the spoils of her second marriage: a young woman, she married her stepson after her aged husband died. My boyfriend says that though it sounds sordid, by all accounts they had a long, happy life together. When he proposed, he said he could have bought a ring, but he'd asked his mom for this one. "Most engagement rings," he said, "have a big stone in the center: it's supposed to be the special part. But this ring has tiny stones all around. Every part of the ring is special. That's how I feel about you. I love your every part."

We tried to get the ring fitted, but the jeweler said the ring was too old. If we messed with it, the stones might fall out. So now I wear it on my middle finger, tiny glinting eyes at the center of my hand.

Many subscribe to this truism: only those who love themselves can truly love others. I submit this modification: only those who love others can truly hate themselves.

After the show, the phone boy approaches, gleaming almost violently. I think of Mick Jagger, how he returned from one of his shows on such fire that he slammed Marianne Faithfull around their hotel room the moment he saw her. I feel my own flames flaring up. I will meet the phone boy glow for glow.

But when he invites us to come back with the band to his house, his eyes betray his preference for my psychic friend. Before she can respond, I jump in. "I'll come by," I say. And then, to my friend: "But shouldn't we get you home? Your therapist says a good night's sleep is key right now." Her therapist has said nothing of the sort. I'm quoting my own, from my last big plunge.

Turning red, my friend marvels at me. I hate myself, but my face forms a Mother-Teresa smile. There's a pause while we absorb the social awkwardness of what I've just done. Then the phone boy says, "Who's your therapist? Lord knows I could use a good one." He cracks a gorgeous grin, and my friend laughs a tune of joy.

That's when I see it: the light weaving between them. It's not easy to behold, not just because of my heartache, but because of the bright, intricate beauty, the nouveau rainbows of shimmering strands. All my favorite colors are there: turquoise, fuchsia, amethyst, teal. Even the kindergarten hues—the standard reds, yellows, blues—radiate complexity and depth. The color combos are garish, in bad taste: not of this world and unafraid. I almost fall to my knees and pray.

Then I see the others. The light cords that bind, their warp and weft: couples, happy and miserable; friends, loving and resentful; acquaintances, lackluster and wanting more. The God field. But when I look to myself, nothing's there. My psychic friend has never, in my years of knowing her, said one word about her own light cords. I'd always figured she was being private. But could psychic-light-cord knowledge follow the same cruel logic of other knowledge: what we need to know most we never can see?

Because see them or not, I know my light cords are there: I feel their tug. My psychic friend's yank and release, the phone boy's constant, inexplicable pull.

And those other fine cords threading out the door, beyond town, beyond sense, into some family's sorry home, where the one I love most tries to gather information that will save them all. I'm almost there with him, breathing the close air of filial doom, smiling over the flagrant or invisible mess, seeking meaning in chatter and silence and stains.

But here, in the coffee place, a shoulder clips mine, leaves a buzz on my skin. I whirl to find its bearer. No luck. And when I return to myself, the cords, those I see and those I feel, be they gift or madness, are gone.

The Men I Love

One of the men I love's pointing a gun at his head, and I tell him I'll do anything if he puts down that gun. This is the man I'm not leaving my husband for. But now I tell him I'm leaving my husband. I call my husband, so the man can hear, and tell my husband I'm leaving him. My husband isn't surprised, but he's pissed. He knows about this man, because we have the kind of marriage where I can tell him about this man, and because we have that kind of marriage, I wasn't going to leave him. But now it turns out I'm leaving him, because this man has a gun to his head, which is like putting a gun to my head: I love him that much. I love the kind of man who will put a gun to his head, and therefore, by implication, my head. My husband, though pissed, will not put a gun to his head over any of this, and I also love the kind of man who will not put a gun to his head over any of this. But it turns out the gun wins. I don't own a gun: my willingness has limits. The man I love's willingness knows no bounds. Life is easier that way, when you are willing to shoot people to protect yourself or shoot yourself to protect other people. When you are willing to leave the husband you love for the man you love or leave the man you love for the husband you love. But now I love this man extra, because his gun has released my willingness, a wildcat fresh from the cage. I tell my husband we'll talk later. I hold out my hand. The man I love places the gun in it, gently, like a pet newly dead.

What Family Does

When my grandfather announced his intention to leave Brooklyn to live with us in Mellisburg, Ohio, everyone but my mother, his daughter-in-law, was surprised.

"No one invited him," my dad said, hunching over his dinner. "Why would he want to live here? He hates small towns. He says they're like living in a lavatory without windows. A *lavatory*."

"I might have mentioned it as a possibility," said my mom, "at Edna's funeral." She scanned us for a reaction. My brother, Lance, ignored her, forking the skin off his chicken.

"Why would you do that?" my dad said. "He doesn't even like you."

My mom closed her eyes, then formed her face into a smile. "He's alone now. And we have more room than we can use."

I expected my dad to explode. It didn't take much for him to cook off at my mom. But instead he said, "Yes," his face straining with the effort of that one small word. He looked at me and Lance. "We have a duty. This is what family does."

I rolled my eyes. At sixteen, I believed that all human ties borne of anything but choice were false and obtrusive. I thought friends and lovers were the only relations worth having, though I had only few of the first and none of the latter. I was pleased, then, when I saw my father follow his pronouncement with a quick sneer at my mom.

"Grandpa belongs with the Addams family," mumbled Lance. Since starting junior high, he'd become an encyclopedia of old TV shows, which he watched incessantly through our new cable television.

"Lance," my dad warned, but his voice lacked edge.

I didn't know my grandfather well, but I'd always been a little afraid of him. It wasn't just that he lived hundreds of miles away and we saw him too rarely for him not to seem alien. At six foot four, with long jowls, stone-gray eyes, white hair combed back from his face, and a slight but unmistakably foreign accent, he was a scary man. When we were little, he never changed his voice when addressing us, which set him apart from other adults, whose bright, tentative tones suggested we were both fragile and wild. I remembered him sitting in a drab green chair that was too small for him in the living room of his Brooklyn home, his knees pointed and high, hands gripping the narrow arms as if he sat inside a lifting airplane. He'd stay that way for hours, staring into space, completely at ease with his discomfort, as though proving a point. He sold carpet for a living, and as I got older, I was surprised by television portraits of salesmen as slick and ingratiating; my grandfather's success at sales, I imagined, was due to a side of him we never saw, or to his extraordinary talent for quiet intimidation. My grandmother, a good-natured, anxious woman, fluttered around him like a sparrow looking for a perch on a large but crowded tree.

A year before at my grandmother's funeral, my grandfather held his head perfectly erect and stared at the rabbi as though gazing at a statue. My mother insisted he was crying on the inside.

"He must have unique tear ducts," my dad had responded, bleary-eyed.

"Well, Laura," my dad now said, "We have a week until he comes. I'm sure you'll enjoy making preparations."

My mother nodded, smiling gratefully.

Whatever my feelings about my grandfather, it soon occurred to me that his arrival could improve my life. Having a project might calm my mother's insomnia, making it easier for me to sneak out to see Dirt.

Dirt wasn't his real name, but it was how I knew him, through the homemade blue ballpoint tattoo of that word on his left forearm, right above his pinball muscles. Dirt also wasn't, to the best of my knowledge, especially dirty. He smelled like blue cologne and wore fraying pastel oxford shirts tucked into tight, new blue jeans. His skin was fair, his hair, dark, and his eyes the same dull silver of the pinball he batted around. Dirt frequented Tiger's Landing, a pizza and beer joint up the road from us that supplied the only food-and-drink service for a few miles. It attracted a broad clientele, from families to teenagers to lone men, who sat at the tiny bar or, like Dirt, entrenched themselves in the game room.

I'd first seen Dirt when I'd gone to the game room to play Pac Man and get away from my family. As I entered, the pinball machine made the popping noise signifying the player had reached the replay score. The player, though, didn't react. He just kept playing. I saw a word on his arm and moved closer to read it. He sleeves were rolled to the exact point above the tattoo. I crept beside him so I could see his face. When he finished, he turned to me. "That's not right," he said, shaking his head. "You got to give an arm's length."

"Sorry," I said. "I just wanted to watch you play." I didn't recognize him from school, though he looked just a couple years older than me.

He backed up from the machine. "Play for yourself," he said. He nodded at the start button, still flashing from his replay. "You can have it. I'm through."

I could feel him behind me. The game ended quickly. When I turned, he was gone.

The next few times I went to the Tiger, he wasn't there. One evening, though, after English club, my friend Mary and I stopped in to pick up a pizza. I peeked into the game room. Dirt was at the Wild Thing machine, his game ending as I came as close as an arm's length would allow. He gripped the sides of the machine and tapped his foot. Then he spun around, saying, "You can't let it make you mad." He shrugged. "I'm better late at night. Your body's closer to a dream state, and your conscious mind doesn't get so much in the way. You gotta come late." Then he plugged more quarters in the machine and played again. I left to find Mary, wondering whether his "you gotta come late" had been an invitation. In any case, I now knew when I could find him and resolved to do so. The Tiger stayed open until two.

My mom's insomnia, however, made any late-night meetings impossible.

My mother needed a project. Without one, she roamed the hallways of our house like a squirrel in search of a buried nut. It used to happen only after she'd been awakened by an emergency call for my dad, but lately her roamings occurred without prompting. Sometimes, to direct her excess energy, she'd try painting in the room we'd converted into a mini-studio. My mom painted portraits of faces torn from magazines. She'd never taken a class. She was afraid she wasn't good enough. "That's what the class is for," my dad would argue, but my mom said art was for viewing, and she didn't want to make people view something ugly. She was a good enough artist, but her portraits always had one ill-rendered feature that ruined the entire face—a nose that made a five-year-old Minnesota girl look like a sixty-year-old Spanish king or an upper lip that gave a Nobel Laureate scientist the come-hither aspect of a teenage songstress. I liked what these mistakes did for my mom's paintings—they made them interesting, unique—but I never told her that. Instead of trying to correct her mistakes, she'd leave them intact, like police evidence in a baggie, and her night wanderings would become more frenzied.

At first, the announcement of my grandfather's arrival did little to channel her fervor: if anything, it excited her more. One night she entered my room and sat cross-legged on the floor, her version of respecting my space.

"It's important you be nice to your grandfather," she said. "Your father loves your grandfather very much, but he's so tense when he's around. We'll have to make up for that."

"I'm not into that be nice stuff," I said. "People have to earn my niceness." Even at the time, I knew the grandiosity of my words. In reality, I was willing to smile at anybody who bothered to look at me in the hallways of Mellisburg High.

My mother sighed. "You sound like your father. Just think of all the lives he's saved."

My mother never argued with me. Instead, she presented breezy suggestions or cheerful diversions that angered me more than disagreement ever could. I remember once, during a fight, my father yelling at my mom: "Stop telling me I'm so great all the time, that everything's so great. It makes me feel like shit." I understood.

"Dad doesn't do it for free," I said. I hated his job. In Mellisburg, it qualified us as obscenely rich. Our large house on the outskirts of town, like some old-world manor, embarrassed me.

"What's Dad have against Grandpa?" I asked. "Why does he get tense around him?"

"Your father loves your grandfather very much," my mom said. "That's what's important." She paused. "Maybe he's jealous. Because your grandfather's so big, in so many ways."

"Dad's not the jealous type," I said. "Remember? He told you to cheat on him. He said it would do you good."

"Cheryl, he was just kidding," she said. "Wasn't he?"

I'd been enlisted to pick up my grandfather from the airport after school. My father was working at the hospital, and my mother feared driving on the freeway. I stopped at the junior high in my parents' BMW, parking it around the corner so no one would see me emerge from such a nice car, found Lance, and begged him to come with me.

He refused. "I can't talk to him," he said. "We have nothing in common."

"You just have to get to know him better," I said, though I was thinking the same thing. "Come on. He's your grandfather." My phony optimism reminded me of my mother, and I decided to switch tactics. After I promised Lance ten dollars of my babysitting money and Beastie Boys on the stereo for the whole ride, he hurled his backpack over his shoulder and, scowling, followed me to the car.

There was construction on the highway, and we arrived at the airport late. Our grandfather stood against the wall at his gate, a leather satchel in each hand.

"Children," he said, with a brief smile.

"Old man," Lance muttered. I glared at him. But my grandfather had already moved forward, his eyes searching the black signs on the ceiling for directions.

"How was your flight?" I asked.

"My flight?" He slowed his steps, considering my question as though it were important. Finally, he said, "Uneventful."

"An uneventful flight is good," I said.

He slowed again, not looking at me. "I suppose." He handed one of his bags to Lance.

"There are way more car wrecks than plane crashes," said Lance, dragging the satchel on the ground.

My grandfather stopped walking. "Yes, Lance, that is true," he said. "But when you get in a plane crash, you usually die. How old are you now, Lance?"

"Thirteen."

"A thirteen-year-old boy should have enough strength and smarts not to drag his grandfather's leather bag on the floor." He strode ahead. I motioned to Lance, who rolled his eyes and frowned, but lifted the bag and jogged to catch up.

When we got home, my mom hugged my grandfather and took his coat. My father reached around my grandfather, both of them bending at the waist so only their arms and shoulders touched. At five foot eleven, my dad looked tiny, his bald head appearing less fatherly than infantile. My mother led us to the table, which, in seconds, filled with food: a roast surrounded by vegetables, salad, mashed potatoes, and homemade bread—wheat, because my mother believed white bread, which she'd been raised on, was trashy. We took our seats as my mother chatted at my grandfather about his room. "I replaced the curtains and the bedspread. They were too frilly. And I bought bookshelves, because I know you like books, and I assembled them myself, if you can believe that."

My grandfather nodded mechanically.

"There's a bathroom next to your room," she said. "I bought you economy-size supplies."

"Laura," my dad said, looking worriedly at my grandfather, "Dad's a grown man. He can buy his own supplies."

"Well, of course," my mom said. "I didn't buy anything personal. Just the basics."

"Thank you, Laura," said my grandfather, nodding her way. My dad's nostrils twitched.

"So, Dad," he said. "When will your stuff arrive?"

"I'm having a couple boxes transported here by the United Parcel Service. The rest, I will keep in storage."

"You should ship it here. We have room in the basement," said my dad.

"That won't be necessary," my grandfather said.

"Then you should donate it to Goodwill. Or sell it. Storage is a money drain. I could make the arrangements." As he spoke, my father's tone switched from stifled annoyance to forced generosity.

"It will stay where it is."

"Just because your father doesn't want to sell all his stuff doesn't mean he wants it nearby," my mom chimed in, looking to my grandfather.

"That's correct."

My father had a contemptuous and dumbfounded stare he reserved for my mother, which he flashed her now, a stare that said, "How the hell did you get here, at my table, in my house?"

"Besides," said my mother, tentatively, "it's his life."

"Broadly speaking that's true." My grandfather put down his fork and straightened ceremoniously. "Our lives are never entirely our own, though, are they? But my belongings are and I shall determine what to do with them."

"Our lives aren't our own? What happened, Dad? I thought you were the last of the great individualists."

"I have done a great deal of thinking in the past year." My grandfather's white brows arched sadly. "I suppose I'm not what you are used to. In any case, complete individualism provides ample opportunity to think about its lacks."

"What's he talking about?" Lance grumbled.

"What I'm talking about, Lance, is loneliness. Do you know about loneliness, son?"

Lance grimaced and leaned into his plate, scooping a spoonful of mashed potatoes, then dumping it back on the lumpy pile.

"I'm sure Lance knows all about loneliness," my mother chirped. "He's in his awkward phase. And Cheryl—she's so driven. Third in her class. Everyone's so jealous."

"Mom," I said, "don't."

"Cheryl has a meal ticket to any college in the country," she crowed.

"That's not necessarily true," my father said. "Some places are very competitive."

"I'm not going to college," said Lance.

"I don't care where I go as long as it's far away," I said.

"We can afford to send you anywhere," my mother said. "Money is no object."

She'd been raised on the poorer side of a working-class suburb of Cincinnati. She enjoyed saying that money was no object, though she fretted over spending it, as if she never quite believed it was truly hers to spend. My parents fought a lot before buying our house, my mother saying it was too expensive and showy, my father claiming it was a great investment, nothing compared to what you'd pay in New York, and certainly nowhere near as fancy, and that if my mother cared so much about what other people thought, maybe she should go marry other people.

"Cheryl still has some time before she has to worry about college," my father said.

"I'm not going to college," Lance repeated.

"That's entirely up to you," said my mother. She smiled at the whole table. "Your grandfather didn't go to college, and he's very learned."

"I'm no example," said my grandfather. "I spent my life selling carpet."

"What's wrong with selling carpet?" my dad asked. "You always said that every job was important, that carpet made a house a home. When I applied to college, you said that people went to college to avoid learning about life. When I graduated from medical school, you said, 'So now you get to play God for a few decades. Don't forget that you, too, are mortal.' Now you're pro-education?"

"I'm certain I said all those things," my grandfather said. "Now I say something else. Is it better I should continue a bastard?"

No one spoke. Then my mother announced, "Someone crushed the Morton's flowerbed last night. Isn't it horrible?"

I waited for my father to launch into his usual response to local tragedies, for him to say, "A crushed flowerbed? In Brooklyn, they crushed your kneecaps. They crushed your trachea." But he kept eating.

"That is horrible," my grandfather said. "Although in parts of Brooklyn, it's fingers that get crushed at night. Sometimes skulls."

"Dessert time," my mother sang. None of us wanted the pie she made. Except for my grandfather. "I'll have some, please," he said, putting both hands on the table like an obedient child.

This began a nightly custom where only my grandfather would eat the dessert my mother prepared, and she would sit beside him, eating nothing, until he finished. My father would go to the family room to watch the national news, my brother would retreat to his room, and I would go to mine, where I'd lie on my bed and imagine different scenarios for my life: what if I'd been born stupid, or beautiful, or exceptionally ugly? I'd stare at the pink and purple curtains I'd chosen for myself at age eight and wished I could remember how to like them. My room bored me, my parents bored me, my brother and my grandfather were freaks. I wanted to drink and have sex but none of the people who did that were interested in being my friend, nor was I interested in being theirs. Or so I told myself.

By now, my mother was sleeping peacefully, and one night, I decided the time had come to seek out Dirt.

Our neighborhood didn't have sidewalks. I walked along the street, and when a car passed, I stepped into a ditch and hiked through the long grass. There was a stretch without streetlights. I found myself grinning, extending my arms, reaching into darkness.

As I neared the Tiger, streetlights reappeared, and so did houses, smaller than where we lived. I'd never before noticed that the Tiger was windowless, like the strip joints we'd sometimes pass in Columbus. Except for Dirt, everything that went on inside the Tiger was perfectly tame and ordinary; was that what the windowless walls aimed to conceal?

Dirt leaned into the pinball machine, poking the flippers at a leisurely pace, his legs crossed at the ankles. He wore no socks with his no-name black sneakers. When he finished, I expected him to turn to me, knowing with his uncanny senses that I was there. But instead he fished in his pocket for quarters.

"I want to play now," I said.

"That's not how it works," he said. He plugged his quarter into the machine. "If you want to play, you have to put your quarter on the glass."

"But doesn't that distract the person who's playing?"

He eyed me hard. "You have to be careful about it. Get in and get out. A little distraction's okay. A good player expects that, maybe even likes it. But too much distraction, that's a real faux pas." As I took off my coat, his eyes, more curious than wanting, wandered down my body. I'd worn snug light blue jeans and a fuzzy purple sweater that hugged my small chest.

"You can play with me," he said. He cupped his hand. I reached for my pocket. I'd forgotten my money.

He shook his head and inserted two quarters of his own into the machine. "You're player two," he said, springing the first ball into play.

We played three times. His scores exceeded mine in not just points, but digits. A couple times, when I lost the ball, he said, "Jesus!" and I could feel the wind of his head shaking in disappointment.

After the third game, he sat down in one of the game room's two booths.

I sat across from him. "So, are you a little slut, or what?" he asked, his tone perfectly friendly. I couldn't tell what answer he wanted.

And I wasn't sure what answer I wanted to give, how to answer in a way that would make me seem strong. I opted for the truth.

"No," I said, as neutrally as possible.

"So you're a priss?"

I knew the answer to that question. "No," I said, this time allowing my voice to express emotion, in this case, annoyance. Everyone always assumed that smart girls were prudish. I hated it. "Would a priss sneak out of the house at twelve thirty on a school night?"

"A school night." He chuckled. My irritation with him was growing, but so was my attraction. He was maybe nineteen, twenty. No male had ever looked at me with that probing warmth.

"Besides," I said, "I don't believe in labels."

"It's okay if you're a slut," he said. "I like sluts. They play good pinball."

"Is that why you're so good?"

"Guys can't be sluts. Or let me put it this way. All guys are sluts, so the name doesn't mean anything on them."

Images of my father, grandfather, brother passed through my head. They were salivating, gyrating, their fingers curled to grope. I suddenly felt deflated and decided to leave. But before I could reach for my coat, Dirt walked over to my side of the table. He placed his finger between my breasts and traced a line up my chest to the back of my neck, ending behind my ear. "You're no slut," he whispered into it. He winked and strode toward the door.

"Wait," I called. He'd gotten too much from me. I wanted something from him. "What's your name?"

"Lyman," he said. I saw a flicker of something in his eyes but then his gaze solidified. He said, "I don't want to know yours."

I avoided the Tiger the week after meeting up with Dirt. He'd unsettled me. I'd thought that getting to know someone like Dirt, an older boy with special talents, would make me feel mature and wise. But our encounter had made me feel young and foolish. His one gesture that might have expressed attraction, planting his finger in the ample space between my breasts, simultaneously pointed out my lacks and increased my wants, an act at least as mocking as it was sexy. And why hadn't he wanted to know my name? Did he not want to know me?

During this time, my father began drinking martinis with my grandfather when he got home from work. They'd sit in the living room and sip at them, tracing the condensation from the glass. My father would speak of his day, and my grandfather would nod, speak of his, usually making a point of mentioning something nice my mother had done for him. I tried to remember why my father had said my grandfather didn't like her. He obviously liked her now.

Once my mother made their drinks for them, a surprise.

"Why would you do that?" my father said. "We can make our own drinks." He took a sip, dumped the rest in the sink. "You didn't even do it right."

Now my grandfather came into the kitchen, his feet pounding against the floor like clubs. "Rodney," he said. "That's no way to behave. I will keep my drink, thank you." He toasted the air.

"Rodney's just tired," my mother explained. "He's worked hard all day."

"Apologize to your wife, Rodney."

My father stood at the sink, the empty martini glass in his hand.

"Rodney," my grandfather warned.

My father dropped the martini glass into the sink, a jingle against metal. "If anyone needs to apologize to his wife for how he treats her, it's you. Too bad it's too late."

My grandfather blinked. My mother looked down, clasping her hands.

My father breathed in, breathed out. "Laura," he said. "I'm sorry. Please join us."

"No, thank you," she said. When my grandfather and father returned to the living room, she clutched the edge of the counter like she might fall. It was one of those rare moments when I wanted to touch her, grasp her shoulder, one of those rare moments when there was enough of her there to grasp. But then she turned to me. "Boys," she said, shaking her head. "What can you do?" She shrugged like a comedienne, then opened the dishwasher.

I began doing my homework in the living room, where I could get an earful, and, if I was careful, a bit of a view of my grandfather and mother's dessert chats. They had little to say. Usually my grandfather complimented the dessert and my mother described what went into it. Then they would fall into silence. My mother would steal a glance at my grandfather, then ogle the table. My grandfather focused on his dessert, chewing vigorously and retrieving crumbs from the corner of his lips with his tongue.

One evening, though, they began to talk. "You'll have to excuse the landscaping," my mother said out of the blue. "I've stopped maintaining a flower bed. If someone crushed my flower bed, I don't think I could take it. I'd rather not have one."

"That's unfortunate."

"It is, isn't it?" She opened her hands. "Sometimes kids will put toilet paper in the trees or soap car windows. That's just a kids-will-be-kids thing. But crushing a flower bed—that seems uncalled for, don't you think?"

"It is indeed."

"My family thinks I'm sentimental. But I don't feel sentimental. Sometimes I think the world is going to pot and there's nothing anyone can do about it. Of course, you can't give in to feelings like that."

"Why not?"

"Well, because it's selfish." She seemed surprised that he had asked. "It's just an excuse not to try."

"I see."

"Then again, sometimes you try and it just makes things worse."

"That's true."

"I'm a very lucky person, though," my mother said. "Don't think I'm an ingrate."

"It's hard to be human," my grandfather said, as though simply observing the weather. "Edna wanted to plant flowers. I told her they were a waste of money. They died, and in the meantime, attracted bees and caused allergies. And the whole idea of trying to bring beauty to a city that had excrement in its subways seemed ridiculous. Of course, I was wrong. I should have let Edna plant her flowers."

"You had your reasons."

"Reasons," my grandfather said, "are the worst excuse there is." He returned to his dessert, scraping up some stray chocolate frosting at the edge of his plate and plunging it into his mouth. "You're a lovely woman, Laura," he said, matter-of-factly, an afterthought.

My mother blushed, joy filling her face. She suddenly looked young and hopeful, as if my grandfather's words had bestowed her with beauty.

It was twelve forty-five and I still couldn't sleep. My mother had crept around for a while but her footsteps finally subsided. For two weeks, I had avoided Dirt. My grandfather's words about reasons echoed in my mind. There were reasons to avoid Dirt and reasons not to. But beneath it all, I wanted to see him again, if only to confirm that I shouldn't. I dressed, crept to the bathroom where I quietly brushed my hair and teeth and applied makeup. Then I sneaked out of the house.

The darkness covering our little part of the world made all our lives seem mysterious and frightening, full of suppressed sorrows and treasured secrets. This version of my neighborhood calmed me—on this night, it suddenly seemed like a place worth living, and I walked that feeling with me, like the train of an elegant gown, into the Tiger.

Dirt was at the machine, bent forward as if hearing its secret. I waited for his game to end, then said, "Hey," as casually as I could.

He turned, looked me over. "It's School Girl," he said. "Isn't it way past your bedtime?"

"I want to play." I'd brought lots of quarters this time.

We played a couple rounds. He trounced me both times, but the second game I kept the ball in play a while longer each turn, traveling some ramps and hitting some bonus bumpers.

"There's hope for you yet," Dirt said.

To hide my delight, I said, "If I spent my whole life playing pinball like you, I'd be good too."

"Ouch," he said. "Well, I don't, you know. Spend my whole life playing pinball." His tone softened. "I would if I could, though."

"So what else do you do?" I asked, breezily, though I was dying to know.

"What do you think? I work."

"Where?"

"Boring," he said. "The only thing more boring than work is talking about it."

I jumped at the chance to be his cheerleader. "You seem pretty smart," I said. "Maybe you can find a better job you like more."

"Get real," he said, with a bitterness that surprised me.

"Sorry."

The darkness passed from him, and he said, with a wink, "I'll let it go this time, since you're cute."

I can't tell you what those words did to me. Dirt's attention had already shifted to whatever he was digging for in the pockets of his jean jacket. But I was reeling. No one except my parents and girlfriends had ever said anything nice to me about my looks.

"I need a smoke," said Dirt, waving a cigarette. He motioned at the big No Smoking sign on the game room wall and walked away.

I followed.

He led me to the gravel parking lot behind the Tiger, tucking himself in the shadow the roof cast beneath the floodlight. He lit the cigarette, lifted it to his lips between his forefinger and thumb, and sucked.

"Can I have one?" Mary and I had tried smoking once. She coughed a lot and hated it, but I figured out pretty quickly how to draw the smoke and keep it in, fan it back out.

He held out his cigarette. "I guess I can spare a drag."

The paper was cool and wet from his lips.

"You like that?" he asked.

I shrugged, trying to convey that smoking was an experience far too ordinary to judge.

"I bet you don't," he said. He took the cigarette back, inhaled deeply, then dropped it on the ground as he expelled the smoke. About half was left. The burning embers made me nervous.

"Why'd you waste it?"

He ignored my question, crushing the bright orange dead with the heel of his sneaker then pivoting squarely in front of me. I could feel the coolness of the Tiger's wall at my back. Dirt poked my breast bone, like before.

"Isn't it about time for you to go home?"

"I do what I want," I said, hoping his fingertip couldn't feel the bumping of my heart.

"Really," he said, lightening his touch in a way that made me only feel it more. "And what is that?"

When I said nothing, he scoffed and dropped his hand.

"I think you want to go home to your mommy and daddy, that's what I think."

"You don't know everything," I said.

"Alright," he said. "Show me I'm wrong."

He leaned toward me, his eyebrows raised, his breath tickling my nose. His blue eyes burned into me. Just as the derision crept back into his face, I grabbed his neck and kissed him. He became a different person, fierce and urgent, all need. He pressed against me, groping everywhere with the grip of someone avoiding a plunge. His fingers dug beneath my sweater, kneading my breasts, prodding my muscles and bones. It hurt and I liked it. I groped him with equal force. He pulled back, unzipped his pants, took my hand and curled it around him, guiding me up and down. "Good," he said. Soon his face twisted into what I took to be pain. I loosened my grip. "No," he gasped, squeezing my hand back over him. Then it was over. My hand was sticky and wet. Dirt zipped his jeans. "Here," he said. He retrieved a dirty napkin from the ground, wiped my hand with neat strokes.

"You can't back off," he said. "You have to keep going until the end."

"Okay," I said, mortified.

"I'm gonna play a couple more games."

He didn't ask me to come along, so I said, "Me too." We headed back to the Tiger, Dirt holding open the heavy door. As I passed, he patted my shoulder. Hope flooded me. Everything would be different now. The arm's-length rule would no longer apply. He'd wrap himself around me as I played pinball, helping me push the flippers at the right time. We'd make dates, and kids from school would see us. He'd drive to my house every night and whisk me away.

Instead, we dropped our quarters into the slots and played as before, in silence, Dirt racking up points with a leisured intensity and I scrambling to keep the ball in play. I ran out of money. Dirt slipped another quarter into the machine and didn't offer one for me.

"I guess I should go," I said.

"Alright," he said, shooting the ball.

"I can come out again tomorrow," I said. "If you want."

"I don't really like to plan ahead."

I started to ask whether I should come tomorrow or not, but he was lost in the game's colors and chimes. I knew my answer.

When I got home, the front-room light was on. But I didn't care what happened to me next.

I walked in to a gathering of the whole family, my mother frantic. She ran over and hugged me hard, her hands climbing my body.

"Thank God," she said. "We thought something horrible had happened."

"*You* thought something horrible had happened," said my father. "She thought someone climbed a ladder to your room and snatched you away."

"You were worried too," said my mother. "You were just about to drive around the neighborhood."

"I knew she'd be back."

"I was so worried." My mother buried her head in her hands and cried, her shoulders jumping with each sob. I felt horrible and hated her for it. Why did she have to love so much? It was ugly.

My grandfather stepped forward. "Where were you?"

"I couldn't sleep. I went for a walk."

"That was a long walk, Cheryl," my father said.

"You can't just leave in the middle of the night," my mother shrieked. "You're sixteen years old. Terrible things can happen out there. To anyone."

She looked small and wild, a trapped, harmless animal trying to make fearsome noise.

"Terrible things happen in here," I said. I almost stopped there, but I saw my father's rapt expression, egging me on. "Dad can hardly stand you and you act like it's okay. You're pathetic."

A large hand came out of nowhere and swatted my face. My grandfather.

"Hey," my father said. "What do you think you're doing?"

The slap hadn't hurt much. My grandfather had restrained himself. But the shock of it stung.

"Did you not hear what she said to your wife?"

"I don't care what she said. You don't hit my daughter."

"At least I did something. Your children . . . your home. Something had to be done."

"That's it," my father said. "You're not welcome here."

My grandfather bowed his big skull. "I see," he said.

"Where's your bravado now?" said my father.

My mother stood shaking her head, surprised and upset, I thought, by what my grandfather had done. But then she said, "No, Rodney, don't. Don't make him leave."

"Oh, pardon me," said my father. "I forgot how much he likes your pies. That should cancel out any child abuse."

"No, that's not it," said my mother. "He likes me. And he has nowhere to go."

By now, everyone seemed to have forgotten what I'd done. My mother's eyes pleaded with my father, and my father coolly watched my grandfather, whose gaze acknowledged no one. I looked at them all, waiting for one of them, just one, to look at me.

"He hit me!" I yelled. "He—hit—me! In the face!" I started to cry, truly feeling, for the first time, the indignity of what had happened with Dirt.

"That's it," said my father. "He's leaving."

My mother spun toward me, her eyes alien and hateful. "It didn't even hurt!" she hissed. "I could tell."

I flinched. My mother had never turned against me like this before. I didn't know she could.

The next morning, I saw my mother sleeping on the living room couch, curled into herself, her hands in fists. When I got home from school, my grandfather and his things were gone. I stared at what had been his room, now emptied once more into impersonal guest quarters, and thought, *I did this.* I felt a pinch of shame, but something else too, something stronger, that made me feel taller than before, and hard.

I found my mother in her studio, painting. My newfound strength left me as I stood, watching, hoping she'd talk to me.

"Cheryl," she finally said, not looking up. "I want to know what you were doing. Last night."

Something in her voice, its lack of typical cheer, worry, or apology, made me want to tell her what happened, but it was too hard to say.

"I was with a boy," I said. Now, I thought, she would awaken, anger, fuss, be my mother again, and I wouldn't want to tell her anything, could retreat into myself.

But she only dipped her brush into a dollop of blue paint and dabbed the canvas.

"Aren't you going to say anything?" I asked.

"Did you have a good time?"

I shrugged, not sure what the right answer was, for myself, or for her.

"You didn't," she said, and she started to cry without noise, the tears streaming down her cheeks. Unlike last night, her tears looked dignified.

I patted her back. It felt strange, trying to comfort this person who had always, even when I hadn't wanted it, been the one to comfort me.

"Are you . . . " I asked, "are you in love with Grandfather?"

She laughed, the artificial light entering her face. "Oh, Cheryl," she said. "Please." Then the light drained. "I'm in love with your father," she said, so softly and sadly I knew it was true.

I didn't know what to say, so I studied the painting, a portrait of a hair-product model. My mother had made one of her eyes too puffy, giving it the inflamed look of a bruise before the darkness seeps in.

"I like your painting," I said.

"I think it's horrid," she said. But in her face I saw, for the first time, a hint of pride, the pride of someone who loves her mistakes so much she repeats them, draws them so close that they become like those photos that enlarge an image's tiniest details until it looks like something else, something strange and intimate and infinitely beautiful. It was that pride I remembered, when, after a couple days, my grandfather returned, and we all proceeded as though no new rifts or understandings had grown between us. And that pride again, a few nights later, when I once more stole off in the night to find Dirt, wondering if my mother would discover my trespass, and what it would cost us, and what we might gain.

This. This. This. Is. Love. Love. Love.

On my thirtieth birthday, I got myself cable. I live simply. I was first in my class in high school, but I never finished college because of my struggles with depression. Now I'm a cashier at a natural foods store. It's a good place for someone like me. The benefits cover my therapy and meds. Plus, management claims to have high ideals. If I lost my shit again, they'd pretend to understand. I'd held the job long enough to afford basic cable, so I finally said, why not? What if life is just about work and money and relaxing in front of the TV at night?

Everyone at Glad Earth gets their birthday off.

"Won't you be short tomorrow?" I'd asked Yvonne, my boss.

"We'll be fine," she said. "Go have fun."

My mom called in the morning. She said my dad was at the office and would call later. She said this like my dad wasn't someone she hated yet was too weak to leave.

I waited for my dad to call. The cable man came and left.

I watched a teen mom turn drill sergeant to teach her girls cheerleading. I watched a man make a dress out of cupcakes. I saw a *Family Ties* rerun with Tom Hanks as Elyse's fun but no-good brother.

———

"So, any big plans for your birthday?" Rick, another cashier, had asked me the day before. Rick had bright eyes, a nature-boy tan, and a sloppy bun atop his head. If not for his good-natured patter, he might have whistled while he worked. But I'd learned he was a recovering addict, and the extroverted cheer I'd viewed as raw confidence now seemed like nurtured humility, an attempt to make good with the world. He had a young son in California he didn't see much. Sometimes, when he thought no one was looking, his face slackened and aged. I loved him then.

I didn't want to tell him that I had no birthday plans, that I'd rather spend the day ringing up customers.

"I'm not doing much," I said. "Just drinks with friends."

Yvonne carried out an organic cake from the bakery. "Happy Birthday, Annie," it said, in bright red letters. Everybody sang, and I'd smiled as well as I could.

The phone rang during an old *Law and Order* I'd already seen.

"Happy Birthday," said my dad. "You're thirty today, correct?"

"Yes."

"Annie Bananie," he said, one of a stream of his improvised monikers for me that rolled off his tongue like his insults for my mom. "Thirty," he said again. "A blink of an eye."

I waited for him to say more: a cherished memory, a question without a yes-or-no answer. Nothing. We'd talked easily once. But my depression scared him. And he didn't understand why I'd dropped out of college. He'd had hopes for me. I'd had hopes for myself. I thought

I'd be a professor, like him, in English instead of political science. I'd wanted to collect and disperse knowledge, and with it, wisdom.

"They gave me a party at work," I finally said. "The bakery made a cake."

"That's nice. It would be nicer if they gave you a raise. How much do they pay you?"

"Twelve dollars an hour. It's fine."

"It's exploitation."

"It's fine."

More silence. I glanced at the free weekly newspaper on my floor for something he might like to talk about.

"Neo-Nazis have been distributing flyers in north Denver," I said.

"So what else is new? When those scumbags stop distributing flyers, let me know."

My eyes watered. I turned from the phone, my throat clenching like it did whenever I felt he'd shut me down.

"How's your health?" he eventually asked: his way of inquiring if I might again stop eating and getting out of bed and start cutting myself and hyperventilating into the phone.

"It's fine," I uttered, for the third time. Was it? I wasn't going to do any of those things soon. I took my meds faithfully and saw my shrink each week. But I no longer trusted "fine"; I'd come to see "fine" as but a respite from myself, whereas depression was the real me, which I battled and fled.

"That's wonderful," he said, too heartily. "And today? You have plans?"

"Just drinks with friends," I recited, the words thick on my tongue.

"Wonderful," he said again. "You know, when I was thirty, you were born. That same year I started teaching at Rousseau. It was a big year for me. May it be a big year for you too."

"Well, I'm not having a baby or becoming a professor, if that's what you mean." I chuckled drily, trying to turn my kneejerk snark into lighthearted wit.

"That is not what I mean," he said slowly, in a voice he used with my mom that said both "I'm the sane one here" and "Don't fuck with me."

"I know, Dad," I said, my heart thumping. "It was a joke."

"Of course," he said. That voice meant "Fuck you."

My throat tightened again; my eyes went wet. "I should go," I choked out. "Busy day."

"I understand," he intoned. "Glove glue."

"Glove glue goo," I said, on cue. Even now, it was our habit to talk this way. It was how we said goodbye.

My dad used to throw me in the air, and when I grew too big, he'd swing me in circles. My mother's gasps were part of the fun. He'd take me fishing, and when we'd come home empty-handed, my mom would say, "Bad day?"

"A great day!" he'd say. "It's called fishing. Not catching fish. Annie understands, don't you, Annie?" I'd nod, understanding nothing but his approval.

I helped him erect a tall fence around our yard. He liked to gripe about the neighbors to me: "the Perkovich woman" was "plastic," a born Catholic who became Episcopalian to social climb; Evan Langton was a lazy trust-funder who'd never move beyond assistant professor; Bob Kapinsky would sell his grandmother to the Nazis and write a book about it. Every time my dad described their flaws to me, I felt, as his confidante, flawless. "Why do you always have to be so negative?" my mom would say. But she was the one who spent half her life hidden in her room, emerging like a heat-seeking missile to find fault with him. Whereas my dad had a full life: an interesting job and, for all his judgments, plenty of friends—professors, students, maintenance staff, fishing buddies from the neighboring town, all people he'd invite over and feed too much. My mom entered the world meekly, her soft, public voice in inverse proportion to her private screams. She smiled and nodded her head a lot. My dad, though, was honest: he kept his distance from those he didn't like or, if necessary, spoke up against them. At one legendary faculty meeting, he'd told a certain colleague to go fuck himself. But those he liked, he gave his full attention and humor and warmth.

After my dad's call, I stared at the old-T-shirt white of my apartment wall for a while. Then I climbed back into my Murphy bed. My apartment wasn't much bigger than the Murphy. When my dad visited, he'd said, "This apartment's the size of a postage stamp." But I didn't mind the size. All the better to return to the womb, a fitting aspiration for my birthday. I could pull my old blue comforter, with its growing set of holes, over my head, and ruminate on my failures and flaws. My therapist said I should give myself permission to do that sort of thing, but to set a timer and get up when it went off. I liked the idea but had never used it. The problem of how much time to set caused me too much distress. I stared at the timer now, thinking, *An hour. Forty-five minutes. No, three hours. No, two.*

Then I remembered my new cable. I turned on the TV and flipped through the channels until I saw a capuchin monkey crashing around a cage. His black-bead eyes tracked wildly. He peeled back his lips, showing fangs.

"Who's this lovely creature?" asked a blonde, middle-aged British woman in a pink suit befitting a real-estate agent. I was surprised when she stuck her finger in the cage and wiggled it. The monkey hopped over. I thought he might chew her finger off. But he held it and gazed at her, his mouth making a small O.

"That's Albert," said a man. "He's been real aggressive lately. We had to separate him from the other monkeys. We're hoping you can tell us what's going on."

The woman nodded and closed her eyes, seeming to inhale a glorious scent. "Is there a young girl with long black hair on your staff?"

"Used to be. Inez."

"Albert's telling me he loves her. He thinks the other monkeys drove her off."

"Now that I think about it," said the man, "Albert started acting up right after Inez left."

"Could Inez visit?"

"She moved. But she'll be back for the holidays."

"I'll tell that to Albert. I'll also explain that the other monkeys didn't drive Inez away and she still cares about him."

The next shot showed Albert frolicking around a cage with the other capuchins.

There was an *Animal Psychic* marathon that day. Evelyn forged a truce between cats. She revealed a llama's wish to be shown at fairs. She reunited a woman with her long-dead parakeet. To a Shih Tzu with a horrendous underbite, she said, "Aren't you lovely?" And I felt lovely too.

After the marathon ended, I pulled from a manila envelope of keepsakes my picture of Banjo, a sweet mid-sized mutt with red and gray patches, who, from the comfort of my family's cushiest easy chair, eyed the camera, his muzzle swelled by the curve of the lens.

When my dad fell asleep on the couch, Banjo would lie on him, rising and falling with his breath. When Banjo got old and lost his sight and bladder control and use of his legs, my dad lugged him everywhere. Even then, the sound of my dad's voice from across the house was enough to make Banjo's tail thump.

He'd brought Banjo home as a surprise when I was nine. My mother, who was terrified of dogs, flipped.

"This dog is harmless," my father said.

"As usual," said my mother, her voice wobbling, "that's not the point."

"I don't want Annie growing up scared of everything. A petty bourgeoisie with a persecution complex."

"Leave my family out of this."

"I would love to."

This was the point when I'd usually slip off to my bedroom and hide until the fighting settled into a bitter calm. But I wanted the dog. From his leash, he watched my parents, his legs taut, his ears and tail raised. My mother yelled and he startled, his black claws clicking against our foyer floor. Then, as if to conceal his fear, he wagged, panting cheerfully and gazing up at my dad.

"I'll keep him away from you," I said. "I promise."

"You can't promise that," she said. "You can't control a dog. No one can. They bite. They maul people. I'm not crazy. It's on the news."

My dad laughed. "This dog isn't a pit bull."

"I know that," she said. "Did I say it was?"

"You implied."

"He doesn't bite." I walked over and extended my hand for the dog to smell, like my dad had taught me. Then I stroked the short fur on his head, enjoying the canine contours of his skull. "See?"

"If I take him back, he dies," my dad added.

"Nice, Barry," she said. "Very nice." Her chin crumpled and she looked at us with those wet, wounded eyes that always made me want to both hug her and run away, and left me doing nothing.

"Come on, Helen," my father said. "Don't."

On cue, my mother cried. She retreated to the bedroom that she shared with my dad but was mostly hers because she spent so much time there, and that's where she stayed, through the night.

I returned the photo of Banjo to the envelope and felt lost. Then I remembered Evelyn, the animal psychic, cooing at the caged little beast, and I perked up. In fact, I felt so much better that I decided to make the bold move of leaving my apartment when it wasn't absolutely necessary. I would walk to the library, sign up for a computer, and learn more about Evelyn from the Internet.

It was the time of day when the sky starts to lose color and the city hasn't lit up yet and people leaving work spill into the streets. I walked in a haze of exhaust and cheap food smells past the screamers and winos and prostitutes on East Colfax. I'd lived here for four years, my longest time in one place since leaving my small Ohio hometown. Before moving to Denver, I hopped along the Front Range, trying to follow a map for salvation: a new school here, a new boyfriend or job there. But it always ended in failure and new or increased meds. Denver was different. I kept my life simple and aimed low. Walking along Colfax, my heart still raced. And not just from fear. I felt like a kid at a fair. Maybe the games cost too much and the rides scared me. But still, a fair! I could step onto a side street and buy crystal meth. I could find strangers to pay me for sex. Everywhere, chances to ruin my life. And so everywhere, chances not to. In other words, as my dad perpetually reminded my mom, it could always be worse.

The problem with depression is people think they understand it. They think it's not that different from plain old sadness. But most people don't understand depression. I don't understand it. For instance, lots of people have a hard time their first year of college. But those hard times don't ruin them.

Growing up in the same small place, I hadn't realized how shy I was. Growing up in a college town, I hadn't realized how unprepared I was for college. My dad had always laughed about big fish from little high-school ponds disappearing in collegiate seas. So I'd expected to feel small. But I didn't expect the other first-years to seem so big. Was it possible they all already knew each other? Hippie chicks hugged like soldiers returning from war. Punks airkissed like socialites. Black-clad sophisticates skipped through the quad holding hands. Orientation disoriented me. We broke into discussion groups: white kids competed for best examples of other white people's racism; soft-voiced uptalkers said "patriarchy" and "hegemony" with the frequency most of us said "the"; I didn't utter a word. My dorm mates hung out on the hallway floor, joking, trading backstories, proclaiming belief systems. To get to the bathroom, I walked over their legs. Sometimes, in an attempt to feel better, I'd drink whatever someone gave me and sleep with whatever boy appeared, but it always made me feel worse. Though none of that really explains why I felt so bad, so often, or why, after a while, I stopped trying to feel good. Or why, by second semester, when what my father had called "my adjustment period" had passed and I hadn't yet adjusted, I stopped trying to do anything: go to class, wash, eat, speak, get out of bed.

My roommate, a pink-cheeked violinist who played ultimate Frisbee and drank prudent amounts of beer with all her new friends, had stopped trying to understand me. But she called my parents, who entered my dorm room the opposite of themselves: my dad wild-eyed and loud, my mother the picture of control and calm.

"You just stopped going to class?" my dad said. "Why didn't you tell me you were having trouble? I could have helped."

This was the man who liked to say to my mom, "Depression?

There's no such thing. Life's hard. You either deal with it or you don't."

I started to say, "You can't help me," but I was afraid.

"No one can help me," I said.

"No one can help you?" he said. "Where are we? Nazi Germany? Fallujah?"

"Barry," my mother said, placing her hand on his arm. "It's okay." She sat on the side of my bed and stroked my hair. I began to cry. It felt good to have her here, to have her be my mom. But why did my misery give her strength? Was it maternal instinct or something else that gave her this beatific glow?

"We'll figure this out," she said. "Figuring this out" meant time off and a new school: University of Colorado, a different world from my cloistered college, a place where I already had a high-school friend. But a couple semesters in, my parents were in my dorm room, having the same discussion while I festered in another bed.

At the library, I'd learned that Evelyn had grown up on a farm, where she first noticed her gift for communicating with animals. A painfully shy girl, she preferred them to people. With the support of her animal friends, especially her childhood cat, Gracie, she grew enough confidence to become an actress, winning roles for British stage and screen. But she felt a lack: she realized her true purpose on Earth was to help those who had so helped her, and *Animal Psychic* was born.

I watched Evelyn whenever I could. Her pastel suits powdered the air of my apartment with a gentle light. And her voice's British music soothed my soul. When she listened to the animals, I felt I, too, might be heard and understood. When she advised their owners, I believed in the possibility of clarity and change. Sometimes after a tough moment at work, Evelyn's image would drift into my mind. "Who's this darling girl?" she'd say.

"What's that smile for?" Rick asked one day, as I was recovering from a customer's tantrum over one ingredient in one natural product that he believed wasn't natural enough. Angry customers scared me, no matter how absurd.

"I'm just thinking about this crazy show," I said. "*Animal Psychic.* Have you seen it?"

"Have I seen it? I love that show."

My heart fluttered. "You watch *Animal Psychic*?"

"Hell, yeah. It's my latest drug substitute."

I laughed. Why did I think only I could be weird and sad enough to love the show as I did? This stupid self-pity that followed me around—I hated it.

"I didn't expect anyone here to watch *Animal Psychic*," I said. "Half the people who work here don't even own TVs."

He leaned across his counter conspiratorially. "Don't let anyone ever tell you TV is bad," he said. "That shit keeps me alive. I'm all for healthy living, but if you can find a way to occasionally kill your brain without harming yourself or others, I say go for it."

"Agreed," I said, fully meeting his high-beam eyes for maybe the first time ever before hurriedly looking away.

"So," he said, his gaze undeterred, "Evelyn. Do you think she's for real?"

The question, obvious as it was, threw me. I didn't think she was for real. I knew she was.

"She seems so real," he said.

"She really does," I said, relieved.

A customer came and as I rang her up, I realized I was shaking. Then I realized what I planned to do next.

"Hey," I said the next chance I got, before I lost my nerve. "Do you want to come over and watch *Animal Psychic* sometime?"

I'd been avoiding men until the mythical era when I would be capable of having a healthy relationship. But Rick raised my hopes. Each week, we watched *Animal Psychic* from the scuffed Goodwill loveseat I used when I closed my Murphy bed for guests. Pitched forward and cupping his chin, he examined the screen; soon I'd find myself pitched forward and cupping my chin too, as if Evelyn had led us in a peculiar yoga pose. Sometimes he'd turn to me and say something like, "Why doesn't the tiger ever say, 'Get me the fuck out of this cage'? They always just want more variety in their diet or someone to sing to them."

I'd laugh. "I'd ask for a chunk of my captor's flesh. Do you think Evelyn censors them?"

"She's got to. But," he'd add in a mock reverent voice, "Evelyn's censorship is never evil and always wise."

Our visits started lasting longer than the show. He told me stories from his using days, which he conveyed with a mixture of wonder and shame. "People think you've gone wild. But I didn't feel wild. I felt more focused than ever. I always knew what I wanted and my whole being worked to get it. It was like serving a God that actually did something: it made you feel really good, and if you forsook it, it whipped your sorry ass. I was the best fucking liar. You should have seen me. My ex got clean before I did, when she got pregnant. I pretended to get clean too. But it wasn't even pretending. It was a total, sincere effort to do what I had to do to keep using. She made me take this home drug test and I was genuinely appalled by her distrust. When the results came back positive, I was genuinely appalled by that. Look how everything, even science, was against me, trying to take what I cared about most. Would you believe that I actually convinced my ex, a former junkie herself, that the test results were false? I did research, I made arguments, I found expert witnesses, I looked deep into her eyes, the whole bit. All that trouble, and then she catches me in the bathroom midday because I wanted my fix too much to wait."

I loved watching him speak at length: he became a flurry of motion, his hands leaping around, his face acrobatic. But sometimes he'd say something like "between you and I," and my dad's voice would break in: "You think you sound smart, but you don't," words he often lobbed at some local newscaster on TV. And in my head, I'd argue, "Don't be so superficial. He is smart. And look how he loves his son."

Rick often talked about Reggie, who loved Arnold Lobel books and wouldn't eat broken food. "At least that's how it was the last time I saw him," he said. "These things change. You wouldn't believe how fast."

"I would," I said.

———

One night Rick banged on my door and barreled into my narrow hallway, shaking his head.

"What's wrong?" I said, anticipation swirling through my chest.

Head still shaking, he held up his palm. "I shouldn't be here."

Why did those words thrill me so?

"I just had a fight with my ex," he said, dropping his arm as if the word "ex" had sapped it of strength. "She switched some dates on me after I bought a nonrefundable plane ticket. Which she knew about. You know what? Sometimes I think she wants me to use. It confirms her view of me as a shit, which then absolves her of her own shittiness."

"Do you want to sit down?"

"I don't want to mess up your show. I should go to a meeting."

"Oh, it's *my* show now?" I joked, trying to make him smile. He did, barely. "You're not messing up anything. Plus, my cable plan includes a DVR, which will be running shortly."

He laughed. "Thank you," he said.

"For what?"

"I like coming here each week. It feels—I don't know—sane. Just watching TV, talking, no drama."

"That's me," I said. "The no-drama queen."

"And I'm the no-drama king." He gestured grandly at my little apartment. "This is our domain." We smiled and then, eyes locked, we stopped smiling. "I should go," he said again.

"You're welcome to stay," I said.

"I can't." He came in for our usual parting hug, and I hugged him back. Whether, after the time to disengage had long passed, I pressed myself against him or his groin found me, I can't say. My therapist, I thought, would not approve. Our mouths met, a slippery union that turned predatory, our lips wrestling until we dropped to the floor for can't-make-it-to-the-bed sex. We fixed our gazes on each other. He looked angry and I felt angry, and it felt good. I thought, *This. This. This. Is. Love. Love. Love.* When it was over, he rested his head on my chest, and a familiar sadness plunged into my gut. I fiddled with his hair, wishing we could stay there forever and wishing he'd get up. One or both of us would soon feel confused. One or both of us would start acting like an asshole. Or maybe we'd make a go of it, get married, and defer all that for later.

He looked up at me, his eyes probing. What did he see? I wanted him to be my Evelyn, to divine what I needed and know what to do.

"This is weird," he said.

"Thanks," I said. The sadness in my belly blossomed. "What every girl wants to hear."

"No. It was great. It's just, you know, I don't want to ruin our friendship."

"Aren't you supposed to say that *before* we have sex?"

"I was a little preoccupied," he said, stroking the side of my rib cage with a tenderness that at once slayed me and perked me right up.

"Well, then," I said, maneuvering my hand to make a low grab, "consider our friendship ruined."

We had a good couple weeks of frenzied sex alternated with good-natured talks about what it all meant. But our talks soon became less good-natured.

"Sometimes I think I'm just using you, like a drug. And you're using me too," Rick once said.

"How am I using you?" I snapped. "What else would we be doing?" I schizophrenically added. "What's this other, better thing people in relationships do?"

"I don't know," he said. "Maybe that's my point."

The sex became more frenzied but also more detached, as if we could make up for emotion with motion. Rick's "I should go"s became "I have to go."

"No, you don't," I'd snip. "You *want* to go." He started griping about his ex a lot, as if she were still a major part of his life, or he wanted her to be. He spent more time at his twelve-step meetings, less time with me. One night I said, "You know what? If you want to leave, leave. Go shoot up or smoke up or whatever it is you do. If I'm just your gateway drug, then save us both some time and go through the fucking gate already."

The next day at work, where we'd determined to keep our new whatever-it-was quiet, I tried to catch his eye to apologize, but he wouldn't let me. So I grabbed his arm. When he finally looked at me, his smile full of pity, I wanted to look away. My chest constricted. Another weird, crappy relationship was ending. So what? Why did I feel like I was going to die? I shook my head. He nodded his. I squeezed his arm.

"Really?" I whispered. "Like this?"

"Let's talk later," he said. "But somewhere public. I don't think we should be alone."

"What?" I yelped. Customers, coworkers, Yvonne turned and stared. "What do you think I'm going to do to you?"

He raised his finger to his lips. "Not now," he commanded, as Yvonne marched over, displeased.

During those weeks with Rick, I almost forgot about Evelyn. Sometimes we'd turn on *Animal Psychic*, in deference to what had brought us together or as a distraction from what we'd become. But Evelyn became what she was, a woman on a TV screen, half remote human being, half particles of light, brought together only in my mind.

Post-Rick, I lay in the eternal darkness of my bed covers, inhaling my own depressive tang, and summoned her. But all that came to me was my inadequacy, and Evelyn's too. Even if she was legit, so what? It didn't change anything. While Evelyn performed her psychic tricks, animals were systematically brutalized on factory farms. And meanwhile, people also suffered a smorgasbord of horrors, many designed by other people, or unconsciously or casually supported by them. My ancestors had fled some of those horrors. And I hid in my bed for no other reason than I couldn't handle my relatively spectacularly unhorrible life.

Get up, I told myself. I didn't get up. I did manage to coax my arm down to the floor, where I'd put my phone in case Rick decided he couldn't live without more misery and dialed me up. I hoisted the phone into the bed and called in sick to work. *Call your therapist,* I told myself. I did not. *At least take your meds.* But they were in the bathroom, on the other side of the globe. Hours passed. I had to pee, but I held it in. Once I stood upright and entered the vast realm of the world, anything could happen. At least under my covers, my bladder engorged but dependable, I knew what to expect. Darkness. Excessive warmth. Quiet, save the passing city-street noises and the constant buzz of my brain.

My brain. My brain. My brain. It was when that buzz got too loud that I glanced at the clock, sat up, and found the remote. The TV lit up, on the animal channel, where I'd left it. And there was Evelyn in an eye-shadow-blue suit, ministering to an elephant. The picture contracted into a perfect square, slid aside, and a new square containing Evelyn, now dressed in watermelon-pink and peering up at a koala, landed center, blossoming into the full screen. "She's been to Africa," a male announcer crooned. "Asia. Australia. And now, she's coming to you. Evelyn Reynolds, the world's favorite animal psychic, is taking her show on the road." More shots of Evelyn flashed by, and then a list of cities and dates. Evelyn was coming to Denver, in less than three weeks. I came to life, hopping out of bed and jotting down information. I rushed to the bathroom and relieved myself. And then I thought, *Okay. This is what I'll care about now. This is what I'll do.*

The next day I showered and medicated and returned to work in complete compliance mode, where I always landed after the darkness had nearly kicked my ass. I apologized again to Yvonne about my outburst with Rick and promised it wouldn't happen again. Around Rick, I was a good little girl. Approaching him with the humblest of smiles, I told him, quietly, that he was right to end things and we should just go back to being coworkers and maybe, someday, friends.

When he responded with a skeptical nod, I smiled humbly again, sorrow burning my chest. At my second smile, his eyes softened, which only made me feel worse. In an attempt to invoke simpler times, I'd planned to ask if he'd heard about Evelyn's Denver visit, but I couldn't say another word. So I got back to work, sensing inside every customer a deep despair.

Three weeks later, I sat unaccompanied in a large auditorium, Banjo's picture in my hand, inside a large, anonymous brown building in one of those liminal parts of the city designed for anonymous brown buildings of general, shifting use.

The building, the auditorium, the picture of Banjo made me sad. Rick had left town for a week to finally visit Reggie. But I somehow hoped he'd appear here, his face lighting up when it found mine. Still, here I was, out of bed, sitting upright, employed. I knew the chances of communing with Evelyn were slim. But I held my passport, Banjo's picture, just in case.

My dad wouldn't like my being here. I'd thought about telling him. But I couldn't imagine that phone call. Besides, what were the chances I'd end up on TV? What were the chances he'd watch? Plus, I was thirty. I could bring a photo of my dead dog to a psychic if I wanted to. My father's dead dog, but still, Banjo was technically mine too. And the larger point was I was tired of the daddy in my head. He was always there, watching. He wasn't even my dad, exactly, but someone bigger, sterner, arms folded, my dad's older cousin from the rough side of town. These days, he bore a slight resemblance to Rick.

At the same time, I held an absurd hope that some words from

Banjo would please my father. Once he got over his initial distaste, he would welcome the message from his beloved and, by proxy, welcome me.

Evelyn's assistants informed the crowd about her special process to choose her "animal guests," as they put it, adding, regrettably, that she could select just a few. Therefore, a half-hour later, it was with great surprise that I followed one of the assistants to the front row.

The woman next to me couldn't stop smiling. Another woman bowed her head over a photo of a parrot, tears dripping from her jaw. Across the aisle sat more chosen ones, people with their living pets on leashes and laps. They were a different breed, these humans. They had that glow that comes with love easily won. I hated them. I couldn't focus on the stage, the featured guests, a rescued Greyhound, an alpaca, the videotaped segment of Evelyn with a gorilla at the zoo. They'd all had, in one way or another, sad lives, but they were in a better place now, and Evelyn would make it better still.

Finally, after instructions from a producer that I was too flustered to hear, Evelyn approached. Something shimmered from her, different from the mechanical TV light, invisible but real, a stream of heat that infused me with such inexplicable calm that I immediately panicked. She kneeled before me in her suit, little hooks of her short blonde hair pointing at her made-up face. I could see the coat of peachy foundation on her skin and the brown pencil lines in her brows.

"Hello," she said, as if she knew me.

"Hi, Evelyn," I croaked, smiling back tears. Don't ruin this, I told myself. Act like a normal person.

"And who is this precious darling?"

"Banjo," I said, my voice shaking. "Our family dog."

"Banjo's telling me he adores his name," she said. "A special person gave it to him. I'm seeing a broad, energetic man, with dark hair and bright eyes."

"My father."

Evelyn nodded, her brown eyes blasting me with love. "Banjo's saying that he and your father had a remarkable relationship."

"Yes."

Now Evelyn frowned. "Well," she said. "Banjo's quite worried about your father. Banjo's showing me an image of your father slumped in a chair. He's been drinking large quantities of Scotch. Sometimes he locks himself in the lavatory and cries."

My seat dissolved beneath me and the floor turned to mud.

"Are you sure?"

Evelyn smiled. "Banjo's sure."

My father crying in the bathroom: this wasn't how the world worked. My mother locked herself in bathrooms and cried, often because of him. I'd detested her for it. Now I wanted to cry: "Daddy, who are you? How can I help?"

"What should I do?" I asked.

"Banjo would like you to tell your father that he's always with him. He wants him to know that his spirit visits your father when he naps on the couch, just as Banjo's body lay over him when he was living. Banjo believes it will help your father to know this."

I cackled. "Well, then Banjo doesn't know my father very well. He'll think I'm crazy."

"Perhaps," said Evelyn. "Tell him anyway."

"Then what?"

She patted my hand. "Darling," she said. "I don't know everything. You'll have to figure that out yourself."

When I got home, I couldn't sleep. I tried smiling at the absurdity of sharing Evelyn's news with my dad, but the humor stuck in my ribs. I found my phone, warmed the cool bar of it in my hand. Then I called Rick, who didn't answer. I imagined him blinking at the phone display and hitting "reject." I wanted to hang up, but it was too late—the damage was done. "Hey," I said, with quivering brightness. "Hope I'm not bothering you. But did you know Evelyn was in town? I saw her tonight. She gave my dead family dog a reading. It was nuts. Anyway, just thought you might be interested. But it's okay if you're not."

I hung up, breathless, and lay there, marinating in anxiety and regret, simultaneously on edge waiting for Rick's return call and miserable knowing it wouldn't come. But just as I was drifting into an unhappy sleep, the phone bleated. Rick.

"My ex is killing me," he said. "I miss you."

We talked regularly for the rest of his trip. And though we paid lip service to proceeding with caution, the minute he returned, straight to my apartment, we got back together. For the first couple days, we were magically better people. I didn't say shitty things. He didn't run out the door. Soon, though, our sincere good efforts became mechanical. I resented not being able to say shitty things. He resented not being able to run out the door. Eventually, I said shitty things and he ran out the door. I believe this whole process took less than a week.

I found myself balled up in bed again, wrapped in my comforter and a closed system of fetid air.

It was then I saw my father, locked in our downstairs bathroom, the walls pale blue, the sink marbled with coppery streaks, the single window covered by a gauzy curtain. I'd always loved that bathroom. It was tiny and private and clean and in that room I felt that I was an honored guest in a pleasant home. My father would have chosen it due to its distance from my mother, who would be in the bedroom. I imagined him hunched over, crying silently, a hand fastened to his eyes like he was holding the darkness in.

White streaks faded his wavy brown hair, and in the soft light of the bathroom he seemed a faded man, his despair mocked by airy curtains and daffodil prints. I could see him so clearly. And I could see myself. My self-absorption. My cowardice. My inability to follow simple instructions from a woman whose guidance I'd craved.

Now I found my phone, my nerves vibrating. I gave myself a pep talk. Of course I'd been tapped to help my father. Who else could help him? Not my mother, who was secured inside her own sorrow and rage. Not his friends, who didn't know him like I did. I was the one. Through whatever channels, Banjo, Evelyn, and the dark authority of depression itself had chosen me. I found my parents' number and pressed CALL.

My mother.

"Annie?" she said. "What's wrong?"

This was a common question from her, and I'd normally bristle. Now I said, gently, "Nothing's wrong, Ma. I just need to talk to Dad."

"Oh," she said. A pause. "Are you sure nothing's wrong?" she said. "You sound strange."

"I'm sure. Will you get Dad?"

Another pause. "Barry!" she shouted, a down-the-stairs holler she'd long ago perfected, half bludgeon, half plea. "Phone."

My dad picked up. My mother always waited too long before hanging up her end. I waited to speak until she did.

"Hi, Dad."

"Annie Bananie."

How to begin? "How are you?" I said emphatically, the way I hated people saying it to me. I couldn't do this. I was going to botch it up.

"I'm okay," he said. "And how are you?"

"I'm also okay." I released a mirthless giggle.

"Mutual okayness established."

"Yes," I said, laughing again, this time with real, relieved joy at my dad's wry humor. I relaxed a little. "So I had this crazy experience," I began.

"Do tell."

I started describing Evelyn and the show, but his impatient silence unnerved me. "It's really entertaining," I said, as if that explained it all, the need Evelyn filled.

"We all need our diversions," he said.

"Well, it's not just entertaining. It's also, I don't know, comforting. Spiritual, even. The idea of it."

"Okay."

"So she—Evelyn—came to Denver. And I went to see her. I

had a picture of Banjo and she gave me a reading." I took a quick breath and spat the rest out: "Banjo said you're depressed. He wants you to know that he visits you when you nap. You made him very happy when he was alive and he loves you very much."

A ragged breath. Then: "Bullshit."

What did I expect? But the word seared. "I believe it," I finally said. I'd been on my bed but now I found myself standing. My whole body pulsed.

"Annie," he said. A warning. "This was televised?"

"Yes. It will be. Soon."

"Jesus."

"I doubt your colleagues will watch *Animal Psychic*, if that's what you're worried about."

"Fuck my colleagues. I'm worried about you. You should know better than to get roped into that sort of thing."

My throat coiled. "I wasn't roped into anything."

"You dishonored Banjo's memory."

"No, Dad. I—"

"You dishonored me. You put me on TV without my consent." His voice wavered, and I thought he might cry. "How could you do this?"

"I'm sorry. I just wanted—" Wanted what? My freedom from him? His undying love? A whole new person to step in and tell me how to live? "I just wanted to help."

"Help me?" he said. "You can't even help yourself."

"That's not true! I'm taking my meds. I'm going to therapy. I'm doing a lot better now." Saying it out loud, I almost believed it.

"Yes," he said. "You are better. And I'm glad you're better. But better means my thirty-year-old daughter lives in a bleak little apartment and sells bean sprouts to hippies and seeks wisdom from psychics and we all rejoice. Until you're not better again. I don't—I don't understand what happened. What happened, Annie?"

I asked myself that question often. But hearing it from him made me mad. "I like my apartment. My job is fine. That's more than a lot of people have." My voice rose. "You have the good job and the nice house. How happy are you?"

"Ah, yes," he said. "My empty middle-class life. I will say this only once. There's nothing wrong with me. The only thing your psychic can see is dollar bills."

"She's not my psychic," I said. "I saw her once. I gave her no money. She knows things about you and Banjo that she couldn't possibly know. You lock yourself in the bathroom. You—"

"Just stop," he said. "You're making it worse."

"What am I making worse, Dad?" I wanted him to admit it. He was lost and sad, just like me. And what he was helped make me what I am.

I pressed my ear hard to the phone, as if it were a shell secreting sounds of a distant sea. My father inhaled. "Your life," he finally said. "This is what happens when people lack education. I'm disappointed in you."

There it was, finally spoken in words. For a moment, I couldn't breathe. Then my mouth opened and said, "I'm disappointed in you, too."

My small apartment, the scuffed wood floor, the dusty TV, the empty walls, the card table I used as a desk, suddenly seemed huge, the terminus of a vast space between us I would always wander.

"Well, then," he eventually replied. "And so it is."

"And so it is."

We hung up. Something inside me severed, and the grief gushed like blood. I bent from the force of it, clutching my waist, and sank to the hard floor, pressing my cheek against it. I stayed there for minutes, or hours, or days. Then whatever it was that saved me, again and again, hoisted me up. I reached for the remote like a lover's hand, and on the DVR I found Evelyn, kneeling beside a Golden Retriever in her studio audience as she had kneeled beside me. And though her counsel had betrayed me, I had to watch.

"I'm feeling pressure in my lower abdomen," said Evelyn. "There's something wrong with Lucy's bladder, and she can't control herself. She's deeply ashamed by this, which causes her stress and makes the problem worse. Lucy thinks you're a great mum and she desperately wants to please you."

Lucy's owner looked stricken. "But she does please me. She's a wonderful dog."

"Yes, darling, but you get angry when she piddles on the rug. She can't help herself. When she piddles on the rug, you must tell her it's okay and you still love her. And you must take her to the vet."

The owner nodded. Lucy propped her paws on her owner's lap. The owner laughed and stroked Lucy's ears. "You're a good dog," she cooed. "Who's my good dog?"

I rewound and watched again, and again. I beheld that small, miraculous reconciliation. "Who's my good dog?" Lucy bounced with joy. As dogs everywhere bounced, knowing goodness: their own, their owners', the goodness of love.

Sometimes Things Just Disappear

The morning after her boyfriend moved out, Sandra couldn't find her keys. She also couldn't find her spares. But because she knew herself well, she'd made a second set of spares. She went through her kitchen and desk drawers until she found them. She added "keys" and "spare keys" to the "Lost" list on her refrigerator, beneath "amethyst ring" and "contact lens solution."

When she got to the parking lot behind her apartment building, her car was gone. She'd parked where she'd always parked. She scanned the other spaces to make sure she hadn't parked someplace else. Her car was definitely gone.

A man sat on a couch next to the dumpster in the alley. He looked like he'd walked through a dust storm to get there. He wore giant glasses with thick black frames and one cracked lens.

"Did you see anyone take my car?" Sandra asked. "A beige Honda Civic. Old."

"I didn't see nothing," said the man.

"Are you sure?"

He looked her hard in the eye. "Sometimes," he said, "things just disappear."

"Cars don't just disappear."

"Mine did." He snapped his fingers. "Like that."

"I'm sorry," said Sandra. She headed back to her apartment to call the police, but when she got to the main entrance, she no longer had her spares.

"Did you see me drop my keys?" she asked the man.

"No, ma'am."

She shook her head. Why did these things always happen to her?

"When you die," said the man, "everything you ever lost comes back to you. In heaven or hell."

"I have to find a phone." She searched her wallet. "Mine's gone. I don't even have change for a payphone."

"Don't look at me."

What now? she thought, stuck in place.

"Go to the 7-Eleven and ask for change. Folks'll give you money 'cause you don't look poor."

She went to the 7-Eleven and got change from the first person she asked. She called work to say she wasn't going. She called her landlord and the police. Then she went back to the parking lot. The couch was gone, but the man was still there, sitting cross-legged at the alley's edge.

"You could get hit by a car," she said.

"Won't happen," said the man. "I tried."

"Oh."

"You might as well sit down. It's easier to wait that way." He traced a circle around himself in the asphalt. "This here's mine. Anywhere else is for you."

"I'm not going to sit in the alley."

He shrugged. "Suit yourself."

Where else could she go? She found a place outside his circle and sat.

"Why are you sitting here?"

He pointed in front of him, and for the first time, she saw it. To the side of her apartment building, a thick, old tree grew out of the pavement, leaning away from the alley as though to avoid getting run down. It looked like it could fall at any moment, but it was rooted, strong and still.

"A leaning tree," she said.

"It's rising. It's rising up."

Sandra closed her eyes and felt the sun on her face. "It's not so bad out here," she said.

The warmth lifted. Sandra opened her eyes. Her hands were gone. She reached for the man with what was left of her. Then he disappeared: glasses, skin, muscle, innards and bone, so that in losing him, she saw all of him. She sat in the alley, reaching. A breeze lifted the hairs on her arms and dropped them into place.

Which Truth, Patricia?

Nathan's driving but it feels like falling, and in the fading day he sees nothing but the road, not the wooded hills or cornfields or farms or the nice new houses on the outskirts of town or the shabby houses at town's edge, and even the road he barely sees, having driven it so many times years ago, the road between his small college town and her bigger small town, between his house and her smaller house, and as he approaches her Nixon-era ranch on a street of like ranches, he seems to float, a parachute spreading as he drifts to ground. Dead leaves, the same sapphire-gray as everything in the dimming light, layer the yard. The big oak. Shrubs. Decorative brick. His mother suddenly dead; his sudden trip home; his father telling the story—"I came home and . . . " —again and again; the excess of flowers and well-meaning people; the ludicrous God-talk from church-going locals; the absurd comforts from professors who believed nothing; the brand-new holiness of his mother's piles of crap; the siege of all the ways he'd been a bad son: all leading here, always here, to Angie's door.

He's here. She can feel it. That opening in her throat; that perfect awareness of her mouth. Consumed by the need to consume. Keep washing. Bubbles sparkle. Sponge whispers against plate. When you wash dishes, wash dishes, Buddhists say.

He's here!

Her sponsor said not to go to the service and she didn't. Because she's learned to be good and careful. Every fucking minute of the day. Plus, how much better that he came to her? Some part of her knew he would. The same part that's been waiting six years for this, the same part that always wants a drink. Then again, she doesn't *really* know he's here. It could be—is probably—her wishful addict's thinking. She should open the door and check. But her mother. Her daughter. Wash the dishes. Bubbles. Plate.

All those years, her mother had trusted her because it was less work to trust her and her mother already worked so hard. Before Nathan, Angie had stayed out of trouble, kept up in school. With boys, just kisses, not sex. If she ever fell in love, she'd thought, she would have so much sex. Sex was the opposite of being abandoned. Had her parents stopped having sex? Is that why her dad left? Her mother blamed the booze. It was easier than blaming herself. In that picture Angie had kept under her bed, her dad wore old jeans and a brown plaid shirt, a farm-boy cap, his feet a good yard apart, making a mountain out of his skinny self. His eyes are shadowed, his grin, huge. As if the grin itself is a joke. On the person behind the camera: her mom. On the viewer: her.

Now she's an adult, so to speak; her mother doesn't trust her anymore and she's glad. Maybe if her mother had been a different sort of person, lazy, happy, unpragmatically less trusting, maybe if her mother had been the opposite of herself then she, Angie, would be the opposite of herself. Would be better.

Once he knocks, it's over. Behind that door, the mud green carpet where, back in high school, while her mother worked, they learned about fucking: how best to do it, and what it could do. Back then, he wanted to be with her always. Even now, thinking about her tiny gasps and colossal moans, her juddering tits, her pleasure-warped face— though he's gotten these things from other women, he wants hers back then, when sex was new and love inebriating and he'd leave her house transformed: no longer just a brainy kid with fighting parents and a wimpy wish to emulate his peers, boys with flat, happy features and violence in their eyes.

How they'd fought, though. Even back when only he drank, sometimes, at parties; she never touched the stuff. But then she started drinking, so much that she'd failed her classes and couldn't graduate. He broke up with her when he left for college. But when he was home on break and his parents would start their inevitable sniping, he'd find himself driving by Angie's. Driving turned into stopping and knocking. The next day she'd break up with a boyfriend, but "not because of him." Then, of course, sex and professions of love, fighting and another breakup. After a particularly long separation, while in the dregs of his first grad school semester, he called her at two in the morning. and she deserted her man and quit her job and left Ohio to live with him in Colorado, where she not just fell but dove off the wagon and he started to hate her. He also still loved her, because he had to: if he didn't, he was either a bad person who'd ruined her life or a lost soul who'd derailed his own or both. But he'd ended it anyway and hasn't seen her since.

Surely her mother's there. And her daughter ("a-dor-a-ble" was his mom's painful report). A thirty-one-year-old single mom, still living at home. Jesus. Turn around!

He knocks.

"I'll get it!" Angie shrieks.

Kayla's in the living room with her stuffed-animal mob. How would Nathan be with Kayla? A few months after she'd moved to Colorado, they'd gone to a wedding in the mountains. She didn't drink, but he did, and made a too-loud comment to his grad-school friends about the irony of weddings: how funny, he said, that such grand romantic displays lead to the banality of marriage. On the way back to their hotel, she asked to stop by the liquor store. He refused. She screamed at him about what "real men" do and don't do, not because she cared about real men or what they were supposed to do, but because it was an easy way to hurt him. At the hotel, he brought a pillow and a blanket into the bathtub and she said just come to bed and he wouldn't leave the tub so she turned the shower on him. When he jumped out of the tub, she tried to block his way; he pushed her aside, ramming her shoulder against the wall. "That was an accident," he said drily. "So don't call the police." Then he apologized: "God, I sound like my dad." She apologized too. "I lost control," she said. "And I wasn't even drunk." He didn't laugh, but together, they found places for the wet pillow and blanket and clothes. "You *are* a real man," she said, trying to make up for before. "You know how I know?" She reached for his cock.

He'd smiled. "And you," he'd said lovingly, pushing her to the bed, "are a real bitch."

The door opens. Angie. "Nathan," she says. Her face looks tired and rumpled, but her cobalt eyes shine. The pink in her cheeks, her haphazard ponytail, her addled smile give her a windswept look, as if he'd met her on a Colorado mountain after a long, hard climb.

"Angie," Nathan says, sticking his hands in the pockets of his unbuttoned trench. He's still skinny, but heavier somehow, in the brow, the lips, the curls dipping against his forehead. His eyes are deep, dark pools, rimmed red.

"My mom died. Did you hear?" He'd meant for that "Did you hear" to have an edge, but it comes out plaintive.

"I'm so sorry, Nathan. Yes, I heard. I wanted to go to the service, but my sponsor thought I shouldn't. I've stopped drinking," she says. Words rush out before she can stop them. She forces herself to meet his eyes. "For good. I mean, I'm not supposed to think that way, because, you know, it sets up expectations and pressures. But I've been sober for almost two years." Ugh.

"That's great," Nathan says—too heartily, he thinks.

"Angie," calls Angie's mom. "Show some manners. Invite the boy in." She wants, Angie knows, to keep an eye on them.

"Nathan Feld," her mom booms. "I heard about your mother. I'm so sorry. Come here." She opens her arms. He hugs her hard. "I know," Angie's mom murmurs, stroking his back.

Angie wants to pull her mom off Nathan by the hair.

Finally, Nathan and her mother disengage.

Should she hug him? Not yet. "Kayla," says Angie. "This is Nathan. Mommy's old friend."

Kayla looks like Angie, with wider cheeks and darker eyes. His coloring. But not. It hurts Nathan to think of Kayla's dad. Even though "he's not in the picture," as his mother once breezily relayed.

"Hi," Kayla says flatly. Angie pinches her face into a smile that she hopes looks like motherly pride. Maybe she never made it to college, but she made Kayla, who's pretty great. Does Nathan see it?

"Hello," says Nathan. Is he about to cry?

"Please," says Angie's mom, removing her paperback romance from the couch. "Sit down."

Nathan sits on the brown-plaid couch where he and Angie had sex. Angie sits on the rust-orange chair where he and Angie had sex. Beside him sits Angie's mom.

"You mind getting me a Diet Coke, Angie?" says Angie's mom. "Nathan, what would you like?"

Angie wants to say, Get your own damn Coke. She says, "We don't have much. No booze here, of course." Her mom frowns. Angie can't wait to drink her regular Coke. At least it has sugar. And caffeine.

When she comes back with the drinks, a silence, punctuated by clinking ice and Kayla's chirps, grips the room.

"So you're a professor now?" Angie finally says.

Ouch. He's an adjunct writing instructor, teaching classes he doesn't want to teach to students who don't want to take them. Nathan's mother always called him a professor, and he'd roll his eyes and correct her—if his father, the professor, didn't do it first.

"I teach composition," he says. "I hear you're a nurse?"

"Not exactly," says Angie. "I'm a certified nursing assistant. Less school, less pay."

"And I'm not exactly a professor. I'm an instructor. At, like, three different places," Nathan says. He grins at her, delighted, for the first time, by his lack of success. "Also less school and pay. And forget benefits and job security!"

"Speaking of jobs," says Angie's mom, "I'm sorry to say it's our bedtime. I've got an early day tomorrow. Angie too."

"I'll be okay, Mom," says Angie. "You go ahead."

"Well, it's Kayla's bedtime too. And I'm afraid that's your job. I've done enough of that in my lifetime." She chuckles. Angie wants to scream.

Nathan stands. "I should get going anyway. I just wanted to stop by and, you know, see how you all were doing, take a little break from the doom and gloom."

Angie's mom hugs Nathan again and says her goodbye. Angie forces back the dirty look she wants to flash her mom: it will reveal too much.

She goes to Nathan.

He's afraid to touch her. Angie takes a sharp breath and reaches around his neck, like she would before a kiss, but her arms drop into a hug. Her head presses into his chest. He holds the middle of her back. He smells shampoo and a warmer, darker scent—her flesh. He pulls away.

"Bye," says Nathan. But his eyes say something else.

Later that night, while Angie's mom snores across the hall, Nathan taps Angie's window. Angie's wide awake, waiting for this tap. She sneaks to the front door and lets him in. They creep to her room. She locks the door. He moves to kiss her, but she pulls back. She takes off his coat, his shirt, his pants. Her eyes rake over his narrow body: collar bone, nipples, penis, hips, knees. He watches her, his eyes wet and soft. "Do you love me now?" she asks.

During the fight that had led to their last breakup, she'd demanded he say he didn't love her.

"But that's not true," he'd said feebly. "I do love you. I always will."

"You *always will*? Sounds like the kiss of death to me."

He shook his head. "I can't win."

"Because you're with me."

"I didn't say that."

"That's exactly what you said. You're always saying you didn't say the things that you say. You think you're being sneaky, but you're not. I'm not as stupid as you think." She cried, that unattractive honking she always released after holding it in for too long. "Say you don't love me. Please."

He sighed, the feigned impatience in his breath betraying real fear. What had she done? *Don't say it,* she thought. He said it. He looked stunned, as if he'd just then realized it was true. He said it again.

Now, years later, plunked back in her childhood room, he says, "I love you. I really do."

She sobs, those same stupid honks. "Where the fuck have you been?"

"I'm sorry," he says. "I was confused."

"You're always confused."

"I'm not. Not now."

"I have a kid."

"I'm aware."

Every part of him feels awake. Even his toenails want her. His liver. For the first time since his mom died, he laughs.

"What's so funny?" she says.

"Nothing." He brushes his hand across her chest. Her lovely sigh. He takes off her sweater. Her face has that wounded look it gets when she wants him. She unhooks her bra. They work together to remove her underwear and jeans. He lifts her onto him and holds her there. Her eyes and mouth open the way they always do when he enters her, as if it's a great surprise. "Marry me," he hears himself say. Her mouth opens wider. Before she can reply, he thrusts, hard.

After, she's afraid to bring it up. Nathan lies across the width of her twin bed, staring at the ceiling, his feet on the floor. She's nestled against him, studying his profile: the burdened brow, the grave down-curve of nose, the sad, sealed mouth—his resting face, even in good times. "I love you," she says, a test to see how it feels, to see what he'll do. She pictures Patricia, her sponsor, shaking her bleached blonde head at her across a restaurant booth.

Nathan turns, pecks her lips, pets her face. "You know what's ironic?" he says. She braces herself, remembering the sadism often hidden in his love of ironies, the bitter glee. "I hated how my mother fed my father's contempt, so I treated her with contempt. She made it so easy for him to hurt her: all he had to do was look at her wrong and she'd scream. When I got old enough to understand, I could feel compassion for her, but ten minutes with her on the phone—I couldn't wait to hang up. And you know what? I knew, I *knew* I'd regret it later, not being kinder to her. And I'd try. But not hard enough. Why, Angie?" His voice cracks. "Do you know why?"

"I don't know," she says. "Sometimes we just are the way we are." Inside her rises a wave of sorrow. Feel it, she hears Patricia say. Face the truth. She hates it when Patricia says that. Which truth? The truth of how she feels now, let down, suspicious, quietly panicked? Or the truth of before, the salvation she felt when he knocked on the door? He who giveth taketh away. But he who taketh also giveth. Which truth, Patricia? And Patricia would say, The hardest truth. The truth that keeps you alive.

"You know what else is ironic?" Nathan says. "Right now, my dad's the saddest fucker I've ever seen."

"Nathan," she says. She can barely get out his name, but she pushes on. "You should go."

"No! I want to be here." He can't go yet, he thinks. That's not how this works. More needs to happen first. "I'm sorry I brought up marriage. That was absurd. But, to be honest, I can't imagine marrying anyone else."

"Me neither," she says. She takes his hands. "But you have to go."

"Is this your revenge on me for saying I don't love you a

million years ago?" He knows this isn't her revenge. He sees it in her face, beneath the sadness and fear—something hard and final. "You made me say it," he says.

"I know."

"You say it. Say it now." *Don't say it,* he thinks. He sees their story before them, an unfurled scroll. Someone laughs at him: His dad? *Your love isn't the Torah,* that someone says. *Try a misleading travel brochure.* He doesn't care what it is. He wants it. He doesn't know why or what to do with it. He knows there are worse problems than its loss and better pursuits than its gain. He knows that what he calls love might not even be love, but lust, immaturity, desperation, deceit. So be it. He'll call it love.

"Say it," he says again.

She looks up at him with a child's eyes, her body curled into itself.

"You can't say it, can you?"

Angie lunges. Sex? Violence? But then she's squeezing him hard. A hug. She presses the crown of her head into his throat. "Nathan," she rasps. "Goodbye."

*

"Goodbye?" Raquel walks into the room and Noah shuts the laptop. Anna would have jumped on that. "Hiding something?" she'd say, the jest in her voice a blade. Not Raquel. She comes up behind him and massages his neck. Then she kisses the top of his head, which makes him feel like a child and leaves an itch he resists scratching.

Good Raquel. Morning sickness around the clock and still a

massage and a kiss for him. "How are you feeling?" he asks, an attempt to give something back.

"Shitty," she says, her smile weak. "Always shitty."

"I'm sorry."

"Well, it's not your fault. Not completely. And it's for a good cause."

Unlike the other good causes in Raquel's life, this one has arrived by accident. "It was going to happen eventually," Raquel said when she found out. "Right?"

For the briefest moment, Noah wondered if Raquel had tricked him, if her care with her diaphragm had been a charade. But he knew Raquel would never do such a thing. Why the stab of disappointment at her unshakeable virtue?

"Right," Noah, chastened by his bad reaction, answered. They liked to joke that after four years together, they were practically married, the humor at once a dismissal of and a nod to actual marriage, as if only by avoiding it could they truly succeed at it. Raquel, whose parents had divorced when she was five, disliked the institution, and Noah, whose parents had stayed together unhappily, disliked the reality. But his dislike contained an ideal, a vision of how marriage should be. Perhaps it was that vision that had made him say, "Do you want to get married?"

And perhaps Raquel shared that vision too, because she'd beamed, her eyes watering, as if she hadn't spent great chunks of her life pontificating against marriage and all it stood for, a stance Noah now suspected had been for his benefit, another fruit of her kindness. She reined in her smile and said, "Why not?"

This is why she's in his office: The invitations. Her artist friend has drawn up a pretty pen-and-ink patch of Boulder Creek winding beside an entreaty to attend their wedding. If Noah likes it, Raquel's friend who owns a copy shop will reproduce it at cost. Friends everywhere: he'd talked her down to fifty guests. They've rented a simple space east of town, less pricey, no Boulder Creek but pretty enough, with a view of the foothills. Her parents and their spouses have already reserved hotel rooms and bought plane tickets. His father too. Three months from now: by then, Raquel is sure, her first-trimester misery will have passed.

Noah examines the invitation, though he already knows what he's going to say. "It's perfect."

Raquel sticks a finger in the air and flees the room. From down the hall, a retch. A flush. The hiss of the sink. She reappears. "Oh, good," she says. "I'll call Devi."

As soon as she leaves, he opens his laptop. *"Nathan," she rasps. "Goodbye."* Now what? Nathan and Angie are supposed to get back together and ruin each other's lives. Where's the full-length story he needs for his book? More to the point: Is it really over? He and Anna? Of course it is.

But after all these years, why write about her now, of all times? Why open that door?

Save his lingering grief over his mom, he has a good life: He's a lecturer at the university, with a three-year contract that makes him the envy of his less fortunate grad-school friends. He has a growing list of published stories. He meditates daily, writes regularly, takes his anti-depressants religiously. He hikes and camps and climbs rocks when he can. Pretty, smart, sweet Raquel: she makes his good life better, no? The baby will change some things, but not that. Maybe he's a little too attached to some television shows. Maybe, even though on paper, he and Raquel don't have cable because television just isn't that important to them and it's the opiate of the masses, etc., the *real* reason he doesn't want cable is that if they had it he wouldn't meditate, write, teach, remember his anti-depressants, or go outside. Because TV on Netflix is bad enough and sometimes all he can think about is that next episode of *The Walking Dead* or *Breaking Bad* or *Game of Thrones* or *The Wire* or *The Office* or *Bojack Horseman*, or, God help him, *Gossip Girl* or *Grey's Anatomy*. And maybe sometimes he can't wait for Raquel to go to bed so he can watch his show. And maybe he wakes up in the middle of the night and thinks about his show, and what's great about it and what's wrong with it and why he loves it anyway even though the best shows are nothing but the best-told lies and why his own stories are full of lies, about something that happened because of something that happened and look how well he tries to write about it and how the imposition of order and beauty on the stuff of life is an exquisite violence, and Anna, Anna Clark, how cruel he could be to her and how he will never love anyone like that again, with all that sweet desperation and raw, ugly need, and how every love thereafter became about not loving like that, about being a smarter, kinder person, about being less alive.

Still, when Noah's mother died he didn't think of Anna. He could contemplate nothing but his own sadness. Anna had come to the service. She stood in line and took her place in front of him, and it was like those movie scenes when someone awakens to a blur that becomes clear. Anna was softer and droopier than he remembered and wore a silver wedding band. He could tell she was nervous. Something fluttered in his stomach and then one of the pain-bricks that kept dropping down in him dropped and crushed the fluttering thing.

"Noah," Anna said, her eyes filling. She hugged him. "I'm so sorry about your mom. I didn't know if I should come."

"No," said Noah. "Thank you. I'm glad you did." As soon as he said it, he knew it was true. The last time he saw her, she was sitting in his tiny, sinkless bathroom, threatening to kill herself with his nose-hair scissors. Not long before that, they'd been in bed, talking about baby names. She'd liked the name Agatha. "*Agatha?*" he'd said. A mean quip rolled into his mind. They'd been rolling into his mind, and sometimes off his lips, since she'd arrived in Colorado, since their big fight on her first night, since the manic "we-can-make-this-work" discussion after, since their pretend-mutual decision for her to get her own place, since she'd lost her own place and had to move in with him. The mean quip that just rolled into his mind was exceptionally mean. He knew what she wanted at that point in her life, and how it had conflated with him, her move out west a doomed mix of nostalgia and fresh start. He'd watched her fill out forms and delete them. He'd watched her fill out forms and submit them, only to find there were more forms to fill, more requirements yet to gain, always something missing. But before they'd started talking about baby names, she'd complained about the sex they'd just had. "It was boring," she said. "Where were you?" He felt ashamed of the boring sex, which was boring because he was tired of her but couldn't admit it because his belief they were "meant to be" was the closest thing to a religion he had. And so, though her dig at their sex hurt his feelings, he apologized and initiated a semi-honest analysis of why he'd been boring, sharing thoughts about how they could avoid boring sex in the future. Somehow, as was the way with them, this turned to baby-name talk. And now he had a mean quip rolling through his mind, a quip so mean yet nonsensical that he had to laugh.

"What?" Anna said.

"Nothing. It's just this dumb thought I had. I shouldn't say it."

"Then don't." Her eyes glinted with fear. This somehow made him laugh harder.

"It's just—" he said. A voice inside him said, *Now!* "You only like the name Agatha because you never went to college."

Soon after, she made him say he didn't love her. Then she closed herself in his bathroom with his scissors. Then she dropped them on the floor and started cackling. "Suicide by nose-hair scissors," she said. "Good god." Then, "I need to go home."

Noah always thought that if he saw Anna again, he'd apologize for everything. But now, his gladness about her coming to the service vaporized. He looked at her pretty blue eyes that clearly wanted something from him and he felt nothing for her, no gladness, no guilt, no lust, which did not prevent him from wishing he could throw her down and fuck her right there on the chapel floor. Another pain-brick dropped. Noah squeezed Anna's hand and, again, thanked her for coming. She kept standing there. Closed for business, he wanted to say. He turned to the next person. At the edge of his vision, he saw her still. He glanced at her, a command to leave. She left. A few days later, he and Raquel flew home.

But lately, when he can't sleep, he replays seeing her at the service, just like he used to replay the nose-scissors night. Before the nose-scissors night, he'd replayed the pre-grad-school breakup, although that technically wasn't a breakup because they technically weren't together. They'd started fucking again while they tried to "figure things out." Sometimes she'd accuse him of using her, and he'd say, frantic to defend himself from the accusation's truth, "Of course I am. I use you and you use me. That's what love is." But then he happened upon her outside his friend's house with his friend's younger brother. The brother took a bicycle from the back of Anna's mom's Ford Escort and kissed Anna on the lips. Even now, he can see them. Even now, his stomach turns.

He pushes a button, deletes his story's last lines. Angie rasping, "Nathan, goodbye": good luck with that, Angie. Nice try.

Anna sits at her computer, as she does on nights when her kids are asleep and her husband's at a gig, and googles "Anna Clark." When she married Tim, she kept her name. Changing it scared her. Maybe she'd mistake herself for someone else and forget she was a drunk and drink their marriage away. But she's stayed sober for five years. And it's getting easier. "Don't say that," her sponsor, Robert, says. "That's exactly what your addiction wants you to think."

Multiple Anna Clarks appear: the Harvard scientist, the Taylor Swift fan, the scrapbooker extraordinaire. Dead women. On page two, there she is: her name listed with an unremarkable time from the 5k she ran right after she'd started seriously getting clean.

Is she addicted to screens? Yes! But who isn't? And doesn't

everyone google themselves, looking for clues to the mystery of who they are and are not?

"Noah Gold" she types. Nothing new there. Lecturer of English at University of Colorado. A 4.2 for overall quality and a chili pepper for hotness on Rate My Professor. Stories published in various journals. One of these stories has a link: it's about a forty-something recovering male alcoholic who finds God and goes back to college and becomes obsessed with his headstrong female professor, who seems to like him until he makes missteps. The first time she read it, her heart thumped: Was she the alcoholic? But where was Noah? Was *he* the alcoholic? The professor? Neither and/or both? If she'd asked these questions of Noah, he'd have rolled his eyes and lectured her on the nature of fiction. "Writing fiction is not *self-expression,*" he'd have sneered. "It is not *therapy*. My job is to create convincing characters and compelling conflicts. Not to parade my neuroses or exorcise my demons. Where am I in this story? Who cares?" And then she'd say, "You should care. Because your story really isn't that good." But maybe she wouldn't have said that. That was the old her. And who knows what he would have said? By now he might say, do, *be* anything.

So when she heard Noah's mom died, she decided to go to the service. Because despite their past troubles, she told herself, they were once important to each other and she wanted to be there for him in his time of need. But mostly she wondered what it would be like to see him again. She entered a big stone church, where all services at Rousseau College, regardless of creed, were held. Noah was with a woman, the kind who never wears make up or nice clothes and is just sort of pretty but doesn't seem to mind.

Anna sat. A young rabbi said something rabbinical. He reminded her of Noah, but then again, sometimes everyone and everything reminded her of Noah.

Other people stood and spoke. The service ended. Anna walked toward the rainbows of Jesus and other figures patched into the windows surrounding the altar and found a place in line. The line moved. Stopped. Moved. And then: his eyes. Black pupils, brown irises, whites tinted red. Black lashes. Tiny pink tear ducts. Noah's eyes! And they were looking at her eyes. Then in them. Then at again. She wanted to say something sincere, but not *too* sincere. She started with his name. "Noah." She thought that would be easy, but tears instantly rose. To hide them, she hugged him. "I'm sorry about your mom," she said. He looked at her blankly. "I wasn't sure if I should come."

He thanked her and said he was glad she did. But then he squinted, as if she were too bright, and looked away. "Well, thanks for coming," he said again. Time to leave. But she couldn't. Noah shook someone's hand. She opened her mouth. There was something very important she wanted to say. But she didn't know what it was. Noah glanced at her, an impatient thrust to his head. She forced herself to go. And even though people around her were crying, she walked fast so no one could see her cry.

That night, she didn't drink, but it was hard. And she didn't call Noah, and that was hard too. She loved the lack of high drama in her life more than she hated it. But still, she'd thought then, and, staring at the computer, she thinks now: Wouldn't it be nice to have some final, adult conversation? Was that what she'd been hoping for at the service? Why wasn't the hug and hand squeeze and lack of hate in his eyes enough? Why wasn't anything enough? Why does one question always lead to the next and the next?

And why is her hand now moving toward the phone? Why is her breath stuck in her chest? Why does that stuckness feel like power? Why does her finger press a number as if it were skin?

*

And why is Nathan/Noah based on a real-life female and Angie/Anna based on a male? And why does Angie/Anna also share many traits with the real-life female but Nathan/Noah share only a few with the male? And why, of the many things that happened between the female and male upon whom Nathan/Noah and Angie/Anna are based, has so much been left out? For instance, why leave out the time that the female got drunk and kissed a boy at a high school party that the male did not attend? Or her subsequent confession and apology to the male, which did not prevent her from drunkenly almost kissing another boy, at another party, before the male walked in? Or that time she came home from a family trip and the male revealed he'd slept with the female's friend and then broke up with the female to be with the friend? And why, the morning she got home from a campout where the male and the female's former friend zipped their sleeping bags together, did the female beg her parents to institutionalize her? And why, instead, every Tuesday after school, did her dad, who couldn't say the word "psychologist" without sneering, drive her fifty miles to see a psychologist? And why, when the psychologist gave her a personality test and told her she was feminine to the point of masochism, did she like the masochism part but not the feminine part? And why, after telling the psychologist about a nine-page letter she'd written the male and the psychologist said, "You must give him that letter," did she not give the male that letter? Why, instead, did she meet her best friend in the school bathroom one morning to chug screwdrivers from Tropicana bottles? And why, after she got caught, did she like being grounded so much, holed up in her room with her small TV every night, taking solace in *Quantum Leap*? Why couldn't she take a quantum leap and not get drunk and not kiss or almost kiss those boys and instead be the best girlfriend ever to the male so he wouldn't break up with her for her former friend? And what about the other boys from that year—the skater boy, the former friend's ex, the motorcycle boy, the frat boy, the other skater boy, and the first skater boy again? Why so many untold stories in just a single year? And why must this story, flung in any direction, hurtle back to the male, as the female herself hurtled back to him at the end of the following summer, feeling extra female as she strode through her small college town in big hoop earrings and a long white skirt?

And there he was, the male, his shirt torn of sleeves, his biceps plumped, his smile aimed at her. A walk to the river, some jokes, some talk, a back rub, a kiss, and they were together again, the past erased, the future unreal.

Let's end it there. Let's pretend we have the power to end it. Let's discard what's to come: the slivers of joy riding waves of turmoil, years of it, on and on and off and on, and then just off, a static now barely audible, now too loud.

Let's pretend I'm telling a story. Let's pretend the story's not telling me.

Knock, knock.

Hello, again.

How have you been?

The Speech

Mother came to our room to give the speech that said always and never and love, love, love. She gave it before she drove to the city. She gave it whenever she thought she would die. She thought she would die when she went anywhere or did anything. When she gave the speech, we stared at our hands so we wouldn't laugh. Our hands showed their bones and veins, like hers. Boys didn't love girls with mothers like her. "Love," she said, her face a cartoon. Everything she said meant fear. The class in the city wouldn't help. She couldn't write or bead or flambé herself strong. "Go away," we thought. She smiled and sat down. Her hair hung like old curtains. Why wouldn't she fix it? We wished we were smoking or talking to strangers. We wanted some man to take off our clothes. "My babies," she babbled. We wanted to howl. "I'll never leave you," she said when she left. We could have lit out; we stayed in our room. We did homework and said nothing of fears: the night, the outdoors, cars, other people. We held love and hate quiet and warm at our chest. Like she'd held us in pictures. She didn't come home. We smiled and felt sick. We joked that she'd gone out drinking or dancing. We imagined a world where that could be true. In that world, we would leave through the window, for kicks. But in this world, the phone: our mother made prophet. "Always," we wailed. "Never. Love, love, love!" And forever after, we wanted our mom.

I'm Dying without You, Tom

Shelly lay awake at three AM in her dorm room, deliberating whether to take her Modern European History midterm at the end of the week, when the phone rang. She sprang from bed, hoping it was for her and not her roommate, Ellen, who was with her boyfriend, Jeremy. Sometimes late at night, after drinking, Shelly would call a boy who'd hurt her and ask him why. She wanted this call to come from a drunken boy asking her why she'd hurt him, though she couldn't imagine who that would be.

But the voice on the other end was female, older, with a clipped, sober frenzy.

"Tom?" the woman asked. "Is that you?"

"No," said Shelly, disappointed. "You have the wrong number."

"Tom," said the woman, "stop playing games."

"This is 425-7717. There is no Tom here."

"Please, Tom. I need you to come home, right now!" The woman started to cry, loud, plunking sobs that hurt Shelly's ear.

"Ma'am," said Shelly, "I'm sorry, but I'm not Tom. I'm a girl. Can't you tell?" Shelly didn't have a masculine voice. She'd always disliked the sound of it, a tentative hum that only sounded weaker, shaky and desperate, when she tried to make it thunder.

The woman sniffled. "You're right," she moaned. "You don't sound anything like Tom. I'm out of my head with worry. You must let me speak with him."

"I would if I could, but I don't know anyone named Tom. There are only two people at this number, both girls. My roommate has a boyfriend, but they usually stay at his place. And his name is Jeremy, not Tom." She wanted the woman to understand that she wasn't lying to her, that she wasn't the sort of person who would deny a request from someone in pain.

"Tom's always been a hit with the ladies," the woman said. "That's his trouble. Let me guess. He's got you under his spell too."

"No," said Shelly. "I don't think so."

"It's okay. You can tell me. I know how it is. I'm his own mother, and he's been in charge of me his entire life. So he owes me. You tell him that. You take your filthy hands off him because his mother needs to talk to him."

The woman's sudden hostility stung. Why were people always mean to her when she tried so hard to be nice? "I'd like to help you, but there's no Tom here. Good luck, okay?" She hung up.

She returned to her bed, not the least bit tired. She got up, turned on the light, then turned it off. When the phone rang, she leapt for it.

"Hello?"

"Tom?"

"No!" said Shelly.

"Oh. It's you."

"Yes."

"I'm sorry. I'm sorry I said your hands were filthy. I'm sure you're much better than the others. I can tell by your voice. You sound classy."

"I do?"

"Sure," said the woman. "At least Tom is moving up in the world. At least he's not rolling around in the sewer with some whore."

"Thanks," said Shelly, her spirits lifting.

"Tom should stick with this for once. I can tell you're worth keeping."

"Tell that to the guys around here."

"If you let me talk to Tom, I'll tell him myself. I'll say all sorts of nice things about you, and he'll be yours forever."

"I swear to you, Tom's not here. I'd let you talk to him if he was." Could Tom be here, somewhere on this campus? "Listen," she said, "does he go to Finney College?"

"Tom at college?" The woman snorted. "Ha!"

"He has the right idea," said Shelly. "I hate it here." It was the first time she'd said that out loud.

"I told him to just get that high school diploma, but would he listen?"

"I have an exam soon and I might not take it. I stopped going to classes last week. I have this scholarship for first-generation college students from Ohio. Just about everyone else here is really rich."

"Sometimes I think he hates me. I love him so much I could die!"

"I can't go home," said Shelly. "My parents yell all the time. Even when they're happy. Being happy makes them madder than anything. I don't know why."

"Tom and I were happy," said the woman. "We were a team. Why can't he see that?"

"Well, he was right not to go to college, at least this one, that's for sure."

"I'd like to speak with him now, please."

Shelly sighed. "You're not listening. Tom isn't here. I wish he were, though."

The woman broke into squawking sobs.

Shelly imagined Tom, hunched over the handles of an old, loud motorcycle that spat black smoke. His jean jacket said Def Leppard and he had long, fluffy hair. Every time a group of Finney students walked by, he'd flip them off, just because. When he smiled at Shelly, he'd expose a chipped gray tooth that made him look a little silly and somehow sweet. He'd hold a helmet under his arm for her to wear when they drove off together.

But a Tom wouldn't get anywhere near Finney. No Tom would come for her, not now, not ever.

"He's not here," said Shelly, "but I might know where he is."

"You'll find him for me?"

"Yes."

The woman cried harder.

"What's wrong?" asked Shelly, a little annoyed.

"It's just . . . no one ever said they'd find him for me before. Everyone else just lies. They lie and lie and keep him for themselves."

"That's just the way most people are."

"Not Tom," said the woman. "He's always been too honest. When he left, his note said he couldn't be around me anymore, that I was driving him bananas. What kind of thing is that to say to your mother?"

"People say things they don't mean," Shelly said. "All the time."

"Do you really mean to find him?"

"Call here tomorrow night. Around twelve. That should give me enough time to track him down."

"All right," said the woman. "I'll call tomorrow. At twelve. And Tom will be there."

"Tom will be here."

The next morning, Shelly got up early and set across campus to wait for Ellen to get out of Psych class. As she crossed Warner Quad, she thought she saw Daniel Mechem in the distance. But she was always seeing guys she'd been with in the distance. She had no idea who they'd be when they got close. Daniel had been a little different than the others. The morning after, they'd sat in the swing outside his co-op and shared an orange. He'd actually called her a couple times. But she couldn't get him to agree to plans, and soon, he stopped calling and wouldn't even return her calls. When she ran into him one night at a party, she asked him why. He said something about not being ready for a relationship. She didn't buy it, so at another party, she asked him again. He brushed her off. At the next party, after slurping down a bunch of Jell-O shots, she pressed her finger into his chest, called him a coward, and demanded he take her to bed. When he tried to walk away, she grabbed his arm, which somehow ended in her tearfully orbiting him until he broke free.

The boy she'd thought was Daniel turned out to be another skinny, stringy-haired white boy in wire rim glasses. Shelly smiled at him, but he looked past her. How was it that on this small, flat campus, where you could see someone coming for a mile, that people noticed each other only sometimes?

Shelly touched the cool brown stone of the Psych building. Ever since she'd read about Finney in her history books—it had a large role in the abolition movement—she'd wanted to be here. She couldn't believe such a place existed only two hours away from her nowhere hometown. But now, touching the stone, she thought only about her parents' gravel driveway, how it crackled whenever her dad drove away in a fury, and crackled again when he returned.

Ellen came through the door chatting with two girls. She wore a silk scarf tied around her neck. Her old sweater and jeans were too large for her, and she looked attractively lost inside them, like her whole body was a special secret. Shelly didn't understand how Ellen pulled it off. Shelly's clothes were always big or small, old or new, bright or dark, in all the wrong ways.

"Hey, Ellen," said Shelly, waving her down.

Ellen looked irritated. "Did something happen to our room?"

The girls drifted off, still talking, without saying goodbye to Ellen, which pleased Shelly.

"No, of course not," said Shelly. "I need your help."

"My help?" Her eyes brightened. Shelly figured Ellen thought Shelly wanted Ellen's Psych 101 expertise. "Sure, Shelly. Do you want to sit?"

It was the first time she'd been nice to Shelly in a while. Ellen didn't like Shelly's constant boom-box blasting of PJ Harvey and Hole, nor did she appreciate the mess all over their dorm room. Shelly promised she'd clean, but she never did. Every time she waded into her ocean of dirty clothes, books, pizza boxes, and papers, she felt she'd drown. And Ellen was hardly ever around now anyway. She spent most of her time with Jeremy.

"I don't want to sit," said Shelly. "I just need to know where Jeremy is."

"Jeremy? What do you want with him?"

"A small favor."

"If you need a favor, I'll help you. Jeremy's really busy these days."

"I need a guy."

"I should have guessed," said Ellen. "Why don't you ask one of your special friends?"

"You know why," said Shelly, hurt.

She had confided to Ellen every fling she'd had and the heartbreak that followed all last semester, until finally, before break, Ellen said, "I'm sorry, Shelly. I can't listen to this anymore. You're caught in this destructive pattern and I'm just reinforcing it by giving you sympathy." Her voice had sounded so brisk and cold. Where was the Ellen who'd asked for comfort after a nightmare? Or the Ellen who kneaded the morning pain from Shelly's neck after a night of wild dancing? Back then they messed up and cleaned their dorm room together.

"I thought we were friends," Shelly had said.

"We are," said Ellen, "but you need other friends. We've been here a whole semester now. I have other friends. I don't have time to be your only friend."

"You're not my only friend," said Shelly, but Ellen had been right. Shelly feared the girls at Finney. They seemed older, more knowing, with their chic, thrown-together outfits and air-kissed greetings and fervent politics. They made her more nervous than the guys did. If Ellen hadn't been placed in a room with her, Shelly never would have had the courage to get to know her. With the guys, at least, she could get drunk and flirt.

"Look, Shelly," Ellen now said, "I don't want Jeremy involved in one of your dramas."

"I don't have any dramas," said Shelly. "I'm sick of them. This is someone else's drama."

"Why would you walk all the way across campus at nine in the morning for someone else's drama?"

"Because I'm a nice person. I care about other people's problems."

"Fine," said Ellen, heaving a big sigh. "I'm meeting Jeremy now. Tell me what you want with him and I'll ask."

"I have to ask him myself," said Shelly. "If it makes you feel better, he'll probably say no, and then after I leave, you two can make fun of me for being such a pathetic freak."

Shelly knew Jeremy would do what she asked. He was a deep, compassionate soul. He wore unfashionably large glasses with inconspicuous rims, and laughed little but smiled a lot, though never without thinking about it first. Jeremy studied French horn at the conservatory, and Shelly, having only known musicians with a passion for guitar, or singing, or saxophone, found his calling intriguingly modest.

One night, Shelly and Ellen had come back to their room with Jeremy and a guy Shelly had just met, Alex, who sat cross-legged with Shelly on the floor while Ellen and Jeremy held hands and murmured to each other on Ellen's bed. Alex started rambling on about how much he admired women. "You create life. It's, like, this amazing miracle. And labor, that takes real courage." Shelly sensed Jeremy's eyes on her. His look said, Are you really buying this? Alex, deep into his monologue, didn't notice, and Shelly returned her attention to him, pretending not to register Jeremy's message. He had been right, though: Shelly eventually had learned that the guys who extolled the virtues of womanhood were the worst of all.

Jeremy waited for Ellen with his French horn case near a neat line of bushes outside the conservatory. Other conservatory students bustled around him, looking harried, but he appeared as rooted and calm as the shrubbery.

"Shelly has a favor to ask you," Ellen said.

"A favor?"

"Don't ask me," said Ellen. "She won't tell me what it is."

"I need you to pretend to be a guy named Tom. On the phone."

Shelly explained about the woman, how she called in the night, and how desperate she was to talk to her son, Tom, who had left her.

"That's very sad," said Ellen. "But I don't see how that's our problem."

"She keeps calling," said Shelly. "You wouldn't know because you're never around. And she's miserable. If Jeremy pretends to be Tom, she'll feel better."

"Won't she know I'm not Tom?"

"She's a little out of her gourd. She thought I was Tom at first. She's so desperate to believe Tom is out there and she can talk to him. I don't think it'll take much to convince her. Just say bananas once or twice."

"Bananas?"

"It's a word Tom uses. As in 'I'm going bananas.'"

"I'm going bananas," said Jeremy, in a voice louder and more feeling than his own.

"If this woman's so crazy she'll believe anything, why don't you just lower your voice and pretend to be Tom?" Ellen asked.

"Because I can't make my voice that low, and even if I could, I'd mess it up. Jeremy's sensible. He'll know what to do."

Jeremy blushed. "Please," he said.

"You're embarrassing him," said Ellen, but her eyes betrayed pleasure at having her boyfriend deemed sensible.

"I guess I could do it. I did some acting in high school," said Jeremy.

"She's calling again tonight. Kind of late. But we can make a party of it. I'll order pizza. And something vegan for you, Ellen. I'll find someone to buy us beer. And I'll clean before you get there."

"Don't you have exams to study for?" asked Ellen.

"I'm not taking them."

"What?"

She hadn't told anyone about her declining grades. With the tumult of last semester, she'd performed erratically, barely achieving the GPA necessary to keep her scholarship. Though she'd been a confident high-school student, now whenever she took tests, certain they'd reveal her inferiority to everyone else at Finney, her hands would shake and everything she'd learned jumbled as soon as the blue book landed on her desk. And papers. A single paragraph could take her days to write until, horrified of missing the deadline, she'd excrete last-minute nonsense. The harder she tried to improve, the more nervous she became, and the worse she did. This semester's grades were already falling behind last's.

"Forget my exams," said Shelly. "What about tonight?"

Ellen pulled Jeremy aside and huddled against him, hissing whispers. Shelly repressed an urge to kick the back of her knees. Finally, Ellen said, "No beer. We're bringing notes for studying. And you'll really clean the room?"

"I will."

Jeremy grabbed his French horn case. "See you tonight, Shelly," said Jeremy. He squeezed Ellen's shoulder, and Shelly felt it was his secret way of squeezing her own.

———

On her way home Shelly saw Pete Chen, a guy she'd hooked up with after drinking too many screwdrivers at an off-campus bash. Pete's long hair was always pulled back in a low ponytail that made him seem at once pulled together and relaxed. Shelly had sworn off embarrassing herself during such post-coital campus encounters with loud, happy hellos. But now, she shouted, "Hi, Pete!"

Pete eyed her warily. "Hey," he said.

She skipped her classes and dove into cleaning the room. She played Ellen's favorite Sarah McLachlan CD in anticipation of her arrival. Maybe she would learn some lyrics and sing along with them in Ellen's presence, to show her they weren't so different after all.

As Shelly tore into an extra-large pizza box, the phone rang. She and Ellen didn't have an answering machine. Ellen was philosophically opposed to them, and Shelly hated the idea of coming home and knowing for sure that no one had called. But she also hated knowing someone was calling but not knowing who. She grabbed the phone.

"Hello?"

"Shelly?" Her mom.

"You have five minutes," her dad yelled in the background. "I'm setting the timer."

"Who died and made you boss?" her mom yelled back.

"Shelly, hang up after five minutes." Her dad had picked up the other phone. "She's gabbing us into the poorhouse. The last phone bill was so high I had to sell the Oldsmobile."

"Stop saying that! You had to sell the Oldsmobile because it was a gas guzzling piece of shit you just had to buy no matter what I said."

"Four minutes," said Shelly's dad.

"Shelly, tell your father to leave me alone."

"Shelly, tell your mother to spit out whatever she has to say before we go bankrupt."

"I will speak to Shelly as soon as you butt out."

"Three minutes."

"Roger, hang up!"

"Don't believe a thing she says," said Shelly's father.

"Hang up!"

"Two minutes." A click.

"God," said Shelly's mother. "He's such a prick. And he's getting fat." She boomed this out beyond the phone. "His belly hangs over his jeans. It's disgusting."

"I'm kind of busy right now," said Shelly. "I should go."

"He got to you," she said.

"He didn't. . ."

"Congratulations," she shouted. "You've turned her against me."

"No, Mom, it's just, you know, I have midterms."

"Nice work, Roger. You're making trouble in the middle of her midterms."

"Back off," called her dad.

"No one's making trouble," said Shelly. "But I have to study. Love you." She dropped the phone into its cradle and picked up the pizza box she'd been tearing, only to find she no longer had the strength. She found a space for herself amid the clutter on her bed and for the first time in a while, she felt almost good there.

She awoke to Ellen's voice. "See? I told you."

"It's better than before," said Jeremy. "Look. There's the floor."

Shelly found the clock. It was after eleven. "I didn't mean to sleep so long," she said. "I thought you'd be here earlier."

"All the more reason to finish cleaning," said Ellen.

"I'll order a pizza," said Shelly, fumbling across the room. "What do you guys want?"

"We want you to clean this place," said Ellen. "That was the deal."

"We already ate, Shelly," said Jeremy. "You don't have to buy us pizza."

"This is ridiculous," said Ellen. "Let's go."

"I'm sorry," said Shelly. "I'll clean now, okay?" She grabbed things from the floor at random and stuffed them into the trash bag.

"You're throwing away your books!" said Ellen.

"Okay," said Jeremy. "Why don't we all sit down?"

Ellen gestured wildly at the room. "Where?"

"There's some space here." He brushed away some debris that had made its way to Ellen's bed.

Shelly took a seat in the space on her own littered mattress.

"I want to leave, Jeremy," said Ellen. "Now."

"I wish you'd stop ordering me around," Jeremy said. Shelly sat up.

Ellen's face pinched with surprise. "Oh," she said. A pause. She reddened. "I didn't know you felt that way. Maybe we should go somewhere and talk about this."

"I'm sorry," said Jeremy. "It's just, this is a stressful time, with midterms and all, and I'm kind of excited to do this bananas thing. It's fun. I don't think I've been having enough fun."

"You're not having enough fun?" said Ellen. "With me?" The pain in her voice amazed Shelly. She hadn't heard anything quite like it from Ellen.

"That's not what I meant," he said. "I'm sorry. I shouldn't have snapped."

"You didn't snap," said Shelly.

Ellen exhaled flamboyantly. "I'm sorry I ordered you around," she said. "I was insensitive. We'll stay, okay?" She climbed on the bed and extracted books from her backpack. "We might as well study."

"I have nothing to study for," said Shelly.

"You know, Shelly," said Ellen, "it's not that unusual for people to have a hard time their first year of college. Some students just aren't emotionally ready. Some really benefit from a year off."

"Doing what? Traveling Europe like you did last summer? I don't have that kind of money."

"There are lots of things you can do. You could volunteer, or—"

"You're really eager to see me go, aren't you?"

"Forget it," said Ellen. She opened to a random spot in her book.

Shelly clicked on the Sarah McLachlan CD.

"Could you use the headphones?" asked Ellen. "I can't study with that on."

"It's your favorite CD."

"It's too distracting."

"Fine," said Shelly.

"You didn't have to turn it off."

"It's lame anyway."

"So," Jeremy broke in, "maybe we should go into the hallway and you can tell me more about this Tom."

"Your music theory exam's tomorrow," said Ellen.

Jeremy shook his head.

"I know, I know," said Ellen, holding up her hands in a don't-shoot pose. "Sorry."

Jeremy and Shelly sat on the hallway floor, their backs against the wall. The carpet, which looked like it came from a budget hotel for people on LSD, normally made Shelly sad, but now she joyfully stretched her legs across it. She told Jeremy all about Tom, how he hadn't gotten his diploma, and how he was a hit with the ladies and tended to be too honest.

"Maybe we should practice," said Shelly. "I'll be the woman."

"Go for it."

"Hello, Tom, is that you, Tom?" Shelly said breathlessly. "Tom, I'm dying without you, Tom."

"Mom," said Jeremy, "it's Tom. I'm sorry I haven't called, but I've been busy being too honest with my many girlfriends. It's a full-time job."

Shelly hoped Ellen could hear their laughter through the door.

Then Jeremy stopped laughing and looked deep into her eyes. Her breath jammed in her throat.

"So," said Jeremy, "you're having a hard time of it, huh? Because if you are, it might help to talk to somebody."

Talk to somebody. Shelly knew what that meant: don't talk to me. The ache of him turning on her too burned her chest. "Who's somebody?" she said.

"Uh, anyone, I guess," said Jeremy. "But I was thinking maybe someone with expertise."

"I hate expertise," said Shelly. Jeremy laughed and the ache in her chest dissolved. "I'd much rather," she said, "talk to someone like you." She tilted her head and gazed up at him the way boys liked, a look that said she was stupid and knowing and innocent and sexy all at the same time.

"Oh," Jeremy said.

The phone. Jeremy jumped up, so Shelly did too. She opened the door, grabbed the phone, feeling the heat of him beside her.

"Hello?" said Shelly. Ellen grimaced into her book.

"Did you find him?"

"He's right here."

"Hi, Mom," said Jeremy, the clip of his finger sending a thrill through Shelly as he took the phone. "I know," said Jeremy. "I'm sorry. It's just—you know how I am."

The woman's voice rose and fell.

"I'd like to," said Jeremy. "But I can't. I have this job. And this great girl. Yeah, that's her. Yes, she's classy. Best of all, she doesn't drive me bananas." He grinned. Look, she wanted to say to Ellen. He's having fun. Because of me!

The woman's voice crescendoed.

"No, Mom. That wasn't a dig at you. You don't drive me bananas, either.

"I know, I know I wrote that, but I was young. I didn't know what I was saying.

"No, Mom, I told you, I can't come home. I just can't right now.

"I already told you why."

He pulled the phone away from his ear as the woman wailed, "Please, Tom. Please!" Jeremy covered the mouthpiece. "I can't tell her I'm coming home, right? I don't think this was a good idea."

Shelly's stomach churned. "Hang up," she said. "Just hang up."

Ellen marched across the room and grabbed the phone.

"Hello?" said Ellen. "No, this isn't Tom. My name is Ellen. I'm a student at Finney College.

"I can't put him on. I'll explain why as soon as you calm down. Do you have a paper bag handy?" she asked. "Breathe into it.

"I'm sorry to tell you this, but the person you spoke to wasn't Tom. That was my boyfriend Jeremy. He was only pretending to be Tom to make you feel better, but it didn't work out. Tom isn't here and we don't know where he is. The woman you spoke to is my roommate, Shelly. She tends to bungle things.

"Yes, yes, I know. I'm sorry we upset you. But it sounds like you were pretty upset before, too. You're clearly in a lot of pain. I would like to help you but I'm not qualified. Your city or county probably has crisis line, which you can find in your phone book.

"No," said Ellen. "I'm sorry. No. That's not going to happen. I hope you get help." She hung up. "Not good," she said.

"Oh, come on," said Shelly. "You loved every minute of it. Watching us 'bungle things' and then saving the day. You'll probably think about it during sex."

"Come on," said Jeremy. But she detected a hint of a smile.

Ellen took the phone off the hook. "She's going to call again."

"God," said Shelly. "Don't you ever stop? I'd rather know nothing than know everything. How can you stand her, Jeremy?" Ellen blinked at the floor. "I mean, really. Psychology? The study of the human mind? What does she know about being human?"

"Shelly," said Jeremy, his face now dead serious.

"See?" said Ellen to Jeremy. See what? What had she been telling him? "Can we go now?"

"But Jeremy hasn't had his fun yet," said Shelly. "Have you, Jeremy? If you're tired, Ellen, you can leave, but let Jeremy stay and have his fun."

"Please," Jeremy said. "That's enough."

"Enough of what?" said Shelly. "Because out in the hallway, I could have sworn you wanted much, much more."

Ellen's face went shapeless, as if waiting for Jeremy to tell it how to react. "Is that true, Jeremy?" she asked. "Do you—"

"No," said Jeremy. "I don't." Shelly could tell that he meant it, and she wished she were a different person, different enough to be the girl that Jeremy might have liked, or to be Ellen's friend, or to take tests without shaking, or to at least help a crazy, desperate woman feel better, instead of worse.

The phone hung from its cord, chanting useless instructions. Jeremy led Ellen away.

Shelly returned the receiver to the wall. Later, when the phone rang, she curled tight in her cluttered bed and let it chime. For hours, the call cried through the night, entering, she hoped, and changing all her neighbors' dreams.

How to Get Over Someone You Love in Ten Easy Steps

Step 1:

Scream your eyes out. Cry into a wall. Studies show heartbroken brains explode later on.

Step 2:

If you are the sort of dummy who needs a human, consider ignoring your feelings.

Step 3:

Fixate on every little thing. Buy yourself spirits. Purchase cocaine. Get yourself into debt. Research shows you are miserable. You may get the urge to feel worse. Be alarmed.

Step 4:

Allow broken relationships to live your life. Don't hesitate to deter your ex from thriving. Snoop. Stalk. Sleep with the person.

Step 5:

Fall into the trap of connection and affection. Feel more bonded. Be especially awful. Cut yourself. Dramatically setting fires, run.

Step 6:

Allow the grieving process to make things too difficult. Spend another day lying around. Feel resentful of yourself.

Step 7:

Give yourself a chance to seek that person out again. Reestablish enough mutual respect so that the two of you can get slapped.

Step 8:

Force yourself on the dating scene. Become engaged to a one-night stand.

Step 9:

Regret every decision. Understand that you are somehow unworthy of being loved.

Step 10:

Take a shower. Comb your hair. Extend your arm to shake hands. Accept that once something is gone, it's gone for good. There is no magic.

Note: This is a found text, mostly abstracted from the wikiHow article "How to Get Over Someone You Love (with pictures)" and mixed with some phrases drawn from Chogyam Trungpa Rinpoche's book Mindfulness in Action *and a few words from a WebMD article on depression.*

Slumber Party

I was a colicky baby, and in grade school, no one wanted to play with me because I cried too much. Through high school, I worried that no boy would ever love me, and then, in college, one did. Charles and I married, and now we have a child, Sarah, who wasn't a colicky baby and doesn't cry more than the average girl. For a long time, these small facts elated me.

My problem started harmlessly enough. Winter had arrived, and our bed was warm. I couldn't think of a good reason to leave it. I'd return as soon as I'd poured Sarah's orange juice and fixed her corn flakes, and had no trouble falling back to sleep.

For a while after school, she'd knock on my door, then stand at the edge of my bedroom as though the carpet were on fire. I'd pat the side of my bed, tell her to come in, sit down, just like I used to sit in evenings at the side of her bed when we'd take turns reading to each other. But she'd shake her head and recite her answers to my questions about her day as though for a grade. Then she stopped visiting, which, I must admit, was a relief to us both.

Charles dragged me to the doctor, who discovered an

underactive thyroid and gave me a prescription for Synthroid. The doctor also gave me a prescription for Zoloft, which I hid from Charles and never filled. In a few weeks, I felt better and that was that.

About a month after my recovery, Sarah arrived home from school, the door opening slowly; slowly she emerged, ignoring my greeting. I knelt and raised her head by the chin. Her immense gray eyes—her father's eyes—were larger than usual, and the bottom half of her face receded, as if she were trying to swallow herself.

"Sweetie," I said. "What is it?"

Her lips trembled. "Theresa Potts is having a slumber party," she choked out, "and I'm not invited." She began to cry—loud, coughing sobs cut with bewildered silence.

"Oh, Sarah." I held her. Theresa Potts had a strange authority over the fourth-grade girls. Taller than the boys, big-boned, athletic, she was nothing like the popular type of my day. Yet, Sarah had reported, all the boys wanted to "go out with her." And the girls, based on the emphatic way my daughter pronounced her name, beheld her with awe. Though I'd always expected some sort of trouble from Theresa Potts, this blatant exclusion made no sense. Sarah was so cheerful, attractive, and social: everything I hadn't been.

Sarah wiped her eyes and squirmed from my arms. "She invited everyone except me," she said. "And Vanessa Bunch. But she doesn't take baths."

"But you invited *her* to *your* party."

She glared at me. "I know!"

I squeezed her shoulder. "I bet you think this says something terrible about you. Don't believe it. This says something terrible about Theresa Potts."

She bit her lip and shook her head. Were my words now useless for her in times of crisis?

"Your father and I love you very much."

She smiled benignly and said, "I know, Mom. I know." Hitching her backpack strap high on her shoulder, she retreated up the stairs to her room, slamming the door shut behind her.

When Charles got home, I was thinking about dinner—whether to make one of Sarah's favorites, chicken fajitas or macaroni and cheese, or something less obviously coddling. She probably wouldn't even be hungry. When Charles burst in, I made a snap decision and pulled pasta from the cupboard. Charles, as always, appeared to have come in from a brisk run, even in his suit. He is basketball tall, and even after twelve years of marriage, each time he appears I'm shocked at the sheer size of him.

"Hey, darlin'," he said, kissing the top of my head. "What's cooking?"

I held up the spaghetti. "Nothing yet." There was a time, early in our relationship, when I shared all my thoughts with Charles, instead of only my conclusions. I'd thought that's what he was there for. But my mind's wanderings worried him: he saw them as insecurity.

When Sarah started preschool, I'd considered taking a job selling Avon to pick up extra money. In some ways, it was perfect: I could set my own hours and, unlike the office jobs I once had, no boss would look over my shoulder while I worked, which always compromised my ability to do the very thing expected of me. I cited all these reasons for taking the job to Charles. Then again, I noted, there was the issue of sales. "All my dealings would be a form of manipulation," I said. "I guess I don't even mind that so much. It's just, you know, some people won't like playing make-believe. They'll smirk the entire time I explain why this red lipstick is in their best interest, even if this red lipstick really would work for them. And they won't say no early, either. They'll let me talk so they can have the pleasure of smirking at me."

"You need to build confidence," Charles broke in. Of course, nothing depletes confidence more than being told you need to build it, but he'd meant well, and seemed so concerned about me that I felt I'd burdened him somehow.

Back when I'd taken to bed, he'd begged me to talk to him. But he didn't much like what I'd say.

"I feel so heavy."

"You have a beautiful figure."

"That's not what I mean. I feel weighed down. Like my limbs are full of sand."

He'd straighten from his perch on the bed. "But they're not," he'd say. "You just need to realize that."

"I can't. You're making it worse."

"Worse? You won't leave your bed. How could it be worse?"

"You can't fix everything," I'd say. "What if I'm not broken?"

"I'm just trying to help," he'd say, before walking out.

Now, in the kitchen, he asked after Sarah.

"She's in her room, sulking," I said, trying to keep my voice light. "A girl at school excluded her from a slumber party. Theresa Potts."

"That's bullshit," he said, sitting down at the table and swiveling his chair toward me. "But, you know, this Potts girl probably just did Sarah a huge favor. Twenty years from now, our Sarah's going to own Theresa Potts and everyone like her."

"Let's hope our daughter doesn't own people."

"Don't be so literal. I just meant she'll triumph eventually."

"Hopefully sooner rather than later."

"No chance of that," said Charles, and, of course, he was right. His stoicism almost cheered me. "But she's a smart girl. She'll deal with it. How about karate? The Jamesons are opening a studio. We just approved their loan."

"Karate," I repeated. "So she can annihilate her enemies?"

"Well, it's not about violence," he said. "It's about confidence." He made a fist.

For a moment, fear flashed through me, that he still felt me weak and, worse, that he thought I'd passed this weakness to Sarah.

"Sarah knows she matters," I said.

"Oh, sure," he said, with a wave of his hand. "But every little bit helps. You know, get her ready for grim adolescence." He stood up. "I'll go check on the victim." But first he went to the cabinet, got out a pot, and filled it with water. I'd been holding the spaghetti in my hand since he'd walked in.

Within moments, I heard shrieks of laughter. I went upstairs. Charles had Sarah by the feet, dangling her in the air as he lifted her up and down. I waited for her to scream "Stop!" but she shrieked gleefully with each lift. Her face dipped between his legs, but she was in no position for her eyes to meet mine, to receive my nervous smile. I went downstairs to prepare our food.

As the slumber party approached, Sarah seemed fine. A little quieter than usual, maybe. But she attended school with no resistance, styled her hair, and even wore, a few days after the news of her non-invite, her favorite outfit: a sparkling long-sleeved tee with skinny jeans, and gray, thick-soled shoes. Had she worn it too soon, it might have seemed ingratiating, desperate even, but by the time she wore it, I could see she still, in her usual way, could please herself. At dinner, she spoke of movies she wanted to see, a college student who visited her class with tales of Spain, cars she would own when she grew up. I wondered if Sarah had forgotten her rejection and would come away unscathed.

Charles said, "Nope, she's hurting. But that doesn't mean she's destroyed."

"Well, yes," I said. "I was just hoping—" Hoping what? What many people do not know about those who frequently expect the worst is that we have an equally strong impulse to hope for the unreasonable best. But Charles was right: Sarah was hurt, but she had her dignity, and would not be destroyed. I wondered why I had reacted so strongly to this: was my problem coming back? Did I need my medication adjusted? Maybe my response had other origins: unlike scraped knees, or a broken toy, or even taunts from little boys in the park, this was her first mature hurt. Charles's response: "Or maybe the other way around. You worry the hurt will mature her."

"I'm not out to stunt my daughter's growth," I said, more sharply than I'd meant to. "I just don't like to see her suffer. That's natural for a mother." I instantly wished I hadn't brought up what's natural. Had it been natural for me to desert my daughter for countless weeks?

"For a father, too, thank you."

"Oh, I know, sweetie, I know. I was just talking about myself."

"Of course you were," he said lightly. "And I was just talking about myself. So we're even."

A couple days later, I received the phone call from Mrs. Brandt, Sarah's teacher, a gaunt, older woman with dyed red hair who frightened me a little.

"Sarah tied a classmate's shoes together. The girl fell and hit her face."

"Was the girl Theresa Potts?"

"No," said Mrs. Brandt. "Vanessa Bunch. Her nose bled but it isn't broken. She's going to be fine."

"That's terrible!"

"Yes." I waited for her to go on, but she didn't.

"I should call her parents and apologize."

"Her parents don't care." She paused, allowing me to digest the horror of what she'd just said. Then: "My concern, with you, right now, is for Sarah. She's never behaved like that before."

"I'm sure she didn't mean for Vanessa to get hurt."

"Probably not. But I'm puzzled about why she would do something like this."

I sighed. "Theresa Potts didn't invite her to her slumber party."

"I see," said Mrs. Brandt, sighing too. "Well, then. Sarah will have to do class chores during recess for the next week. And write an apology to Vanessa. I'm going to talk to her about finding more constructive ways of expressing herself. It would be helpful if you and your husband would talk to her as well."

"We do talk to her. We talk to her all the time."

"I'm sure you do," said Mrs. Brandt, as though she knew of my desertion.

When Sarah got home from school, I gripped her shoulders and waited for her to speak.

"I'm fine, Mom," she said sharply, breaking free from my grasp.

"Why Vanessa Bunch?"

She shrugged. "It was just a joke. I didn't mean for her to fall."

"You tied her shoes together. What did you think would happen?"

"It's her own fault. She didn't even notice what I was doing. She's such a space case."

"That's not the way to handle this."

"Handle what?"

"Not being invited to the party."

She scowled. "My punishment's dumb. I have to miss recess for the next week, and I'm glad."

"Well, then, I'm sure we can come up with a better punishment."

"You're too stupid."

I was too shocked to yell. I had a quick vision of slapping her, but I restrained my hand.

"I know I'm not perfect," I said. "I know I haven't been—It's important you use things like this to become a better person, not a worse one."

"I am a better person. I'm better than Vanessa Bunch." She marched to her room before I could send her there.

Charles said he'd talk to her. I waited for the sound of her door closing behind him and then I sneaked upstairs. But before I even reached the door, I heard the laughter Sarah reserved for her father. And then, her tears.

"I just saw someone tie shoes together on TV. It was funny. I didn't mean to hurt her."

"Well, now you know to think about the consequences of your actions. You've learned an important lesson."

"I have to miss recess," she said. "And Mom wants to punish me, too. I deserve to be punished."

"Easy now," said Charles. "I think we've had enough melodrama around here for a while. I'll talk to your mother."

I almost opened the door to ask Sarah which parent she really thought was stupid. But listening at my daughter's door—neither of them would forgive me. So instead, I banged on the dark wood.

"What?" Sarah snipped.

I opened the door. "I don't feel like cooking tonight."

"Fine," said Charles. "We'll get pizza."

Sarah's face lit up.

"I'm not in the mood for pizza," I said.

"Then burgers," said Charles. "I'll take care of it."

They looked at me impatiently. I shut the door, closed them in again.

Later, in bed, Charles spoke to me about not dealing Sarah her punishment.

"She's your daughter," I said. "Do what you want."

"Are you disowning her now?"

"Of course not," I said. "That's a terrible thing to say."

"I didn't say it," he said. "You did."

"That's not what I said." I wanted nothing more than to end this conversation. "You're right," I relented. "She's been punished enough."

The night of the slumber party, Charles and I had planned an evening out, a resumption of our monthly date night, which had lapsed during my sickness. But I now suggested cancelling: we could stay home with Sarah, watch Netflix, eat popcorn, and squirt Hershey's syrup into our Cokes.

Charles refused: "You need to get out of the house. Besides, she doesn't want your pity."

"I suppose she only wants yours," I muttered.

"That wasn't pity. It was rationality." His eyes raked over my T-shirt and jeans. "Get dressed."

We invited Jessi, our fifteen-year-old neighbor, to stay with

Sarah. Sarah adored Jessi, and Jessi always treated Sarah as a friend: she hardly knew she was being babysat.

When Jessi arrived, I pulled her aside and told her about the slumber party, and to make extra sure Sarah had a good time tonight, and that she could stay up later than usual.

Jessi nodded vigorously. "I know how it is," she said, in a peppy way that made me think she didn't, at all.

Charles had made reservations at his favorite restaurant, Massey's, one of the only places in Mellisburg that courted elegance. I didn't love Massey's. The ornate chandeliers, the crimson carpet, the gilded mirrors on the wall were much too much, and the food, like the decor, was often overdone. But I had to give them points for trying, the nervous way the servers uncorked the wine, and the apologetic looks when they laid down the bill. The owner, George Massey, took a genuine interest in his customers' pleasure, and when he made his rounds, I always told him the food was marvelous, in hopes it one day would be.

The waiter brought wine to the table—a Merlot. I hadn't heard Charles order it.

"Do you think she's going to be okay with Jessi?" I asked. "Jessi's just so, I don't know, well adjusted."

"You'd rather we left her with an ax murderer?"

"Of course not. I'm just not sure Jessi really understands what Sarah's going through tonight."

Charles exhaled, less a sigh than hiss, and poured himself more wine.

"I really would have preferred Chardonnay," I said. "You didn't even ask."

"I did ask. You weren't paying attention."

"I guess I'm just worried. About Sarah."

"No kidding. But you don't have to be. I think you think you have to. I think you think you have something to prove."

"That's not it, Charles. It's just so sad. That first rejection. Nothing's the same after that."

He drummed his fingers, the sound muted by the cheap off-white tablecloth. He drank water. His avoidance of my eyes made him easy to watch but hard to discern. Finally, he said, "Sometimes I'd get in bed with you. During the day. The bed was so warm. Your skin was almost too hot to touch. You barely noticed I was there. You just thought it was night, I guess."

"Charles," I said. "It wasn't about you. I'm not really sure what it was about. I mean, my thyroid wasn't working. And I just stopped working. It was a mechanical difficulty. But it wasn't about you."

"I know it wasn't," he said. He sipped his wine carefully, and I sipped mine too.

When we got home, Sarah was sitting beside Jessi on the couch, eating ice cream from the carton and watching a concert performed by a nondescript, lithesome teenage girl. The songstress wagged her finger and gyrated her hips.

"How was your evening?" I asked.

"Shhh," said Sarah. "We're watching."

Jessi smiled apologetically.

"Well," I said lightly, in a softer voice, "you're obviously having a good time now."

"I said, 'Quiet'!" Sarah turned to me, her eyes spilling hate.

"Sarah," Charles warned.

"Sorry," she said to him.

I sat down and watched the show. I enjoyed seeing the singer's face strain for the high notes. She was beginning to sweat.

A few days later, Sarah announced she was having a friend over after school. I asked whom, and she said, with a casualness that had to be forced, "Theresa."

"Theresa Potts?" I asked, though I knew there were no other Theresas who counted.

"Um-hmm."

"Please tell me what foolishness led you to invite that girl here."

Sarah shrugged. "She wants to download some of my music."

"Then she's using you. Do you know what that means?"

"It was my idea."

"Well," I said. "It's a bad one."

She shrugged again.

"She doesn't even like you, Sarah. You want to bring her into this house?"

She exhaled, hard. "How do you know if she likes me or not? You're not a mind reader. You think you know everything, but you don't."

"I don't think I know everything," I said. "It sounds like you're the one who's jumping to conclusions."

Again, she shrugged.

I mimicked her, shrugging frantically. "All those brains, and that's the best you can come up with."

She smiled and shrugged once more, very slowly.

"Tell Theresa Potts she can't come. You have other plans."

"I'm not allowed to lie," she said.

"Then tell her she isn't welcome here."

"I'm not supposed to be rude," she said, clearly enjoying herself.

"I hereby lift the rules. Lie or be rude. Or when she gets here, I will. Or worse. If she comes through that door, I will find a way to embarrass you."

"No, you won't," she said. "Dad won't let you."

When I told Charles that Sarah had invited Theresa Potts to our home, he said, "Of course she did."

"I don't want her to be the kind of girl who lets people walk all over her."

"Let her make her own choices, then."

"How long are you two going to hate me?"

"No one hates you, Karen. You need to make peace with yourself."

The next day after school, Sarah entered the house with Theresa Potts behind her. Sarah was doing all the talking and Theresa looked bored. She was gangly, almost my height, and once again I scrutinized her for something remarkable to explain her appeal. Her shirt sleeves contained outlines of biceps. Her eyes were light, almost clear—her best feature. The rest of her face had a spongy, shapeless quality, and she was extremely pale.

"Mrs. Brandt's a total stick," said Sarah. "If she turns to the side, she practically disappears, right?"

Theresa smiled slowly, giving Sarah a sidelong glance. It was hard to tell if she was appreciating or scorning her.

"Hello, Theresa," I said.

"Hey." Her eyes grazed across the kitchen, and I was suddenly aware of its colors: the faded green and white of the linoleum, the lime curtains pulled back from the window above the sink. Sarah looked pleadingly at me. I liked it.

"Theresa," I said, with a long pause. "Would you like something to drink?"

"A Pepsi."

"We don't have Pepsi, just Coke."

"I don't want anything then." At first I thought she was kidding. She wasn't.

Just then Charles came in, the screen door crashing shut behind him. He'd had a meeting that day and was home early.

He marched over to Theresa and stuck out his hand. "Good to see you," he said. She watched it for a moment before taking it.

"Sarah." He patted her head. She looked miserable. "Why the long face?" She ignored him. He threw her over his shoulder, then flipped her upside down.

"Stop," Sarah shouted. "Dad, stop." He put her back on her feet.

"If you hang upside down for too long, you die," said Theresa.

"Settle down, everyone. I'm not out to murder my daughter."

"Theresa can do a handstand longer than anyone," said Sarah. "A headstand too."

"We'd love to see," said Charles.

"It's not a big deal." She was deprecating us, not herself.

"Show us," I said. If she were doing a handstand, she probably wouldn't talk. I led her to the living room. Charles and Sarah followed.

Theresa took off her shoes. She raised her arms, took a breath, then launched her feet in the air, pointing her toes. I could feel the lift, as though I'd done it myself. I used to do it. At school, on the playground, I couldn't cartwheel or back walkover or even backbend, but I could stand on my hands. What a release, that miraculous shifting of weight.

After a time, Theresa threatened to fall, and she adjusted her hands, regaining balance. She seemed invincible, holding herself up like that. I envied her, this wan, gangly ten-year-old girl. My hatred swelled, and I itched to kick her in the face, an urge so horrifying I did the only thing I could think of to distract myself. I stepped forward and pushed her leg, not hard, but just enough to ruin her equilibrium.

Sarah and Charles let out cries as Theresa toppled to the floor. She got to her feet, her face flushed.

"What the hell?" she said.

"I—I'm sorry. It was an accident." I answered. "I just …" I

looked at the hostile faces surrounding me and knew there was no way I could explain.

"Are you okay, Theresa?" asked Charles.

"Yeah," she said. She turned to Sarah. "Your mom's a psycho."

"I know," said Sarah. "I'm sorry."

"I'm out of here."

Sarah went after her. "Don't go," she said. They left the house. I started to go after Sarah, but Charles grabbed my arm.

"You've done enough. You're lucky she wasn't hurt. What's wrong with you?"

"Sarah shouldn't have brought her here."

"Don't put this on Sarah. You humiliated her."

"She humiliated herself," I said. "She still is. Chasing that girl."

Charles and I stared at each other, then Charles looked away, his expression laced with disgust. "Karen," he said. "We need to talk." He sat on the sofa. "Now."

I headed for a chair, ready to talk and listen, deflect and plea. But something stopped me. The expanse of carpet below, rough but soft, inviting.

I tucked my blouse into my pants, poised my arms, kicked up a leg and I was off, down and up in the right places, Charles ejected from view.

But then, the inevitable. My legs started teetering. I scissored them this way and that, grasping at balance. And when Sarah returned, alone, that's how she found me.

Median

She had just fed the baby and she had to get home to feed the baby. The light wouldn't change. The man on the median held a sign that said, "X-marine needs help." She'd spent a hundred and twenty-four dollars and hadn't bought what she'd gone to the store for. The man had comb lines in his hair. She decided to meet his eyes, but he scanned the cars in front of her. She could tell the people in those cars had great lives. They had more money and friends than she did. They had a clear sense of purpose and great careers. They had babies who slept through the night and napped and didn't need to be held every second. They didn't have prediabetes or a thyroid condition or a bad memory or clogged milk ducts or thinning hair or irritable bowels or insomnia or the frequent urge to urinate or a great husband whose touch made them cringe or a two-year-old who constantly asked, "Are you happy?" and cried if they didn't say, "Yes."

She dug into her purse. She hoped the people in front of her saw the man limp over to take her bill.

"God bless you," he said, resting his hand where the window would raise.

"You too." She couldn't say God.

The man smiled. His teeth were straight and stained. He was too old for this Iraq war. Maybe he'd gone to the first one.

Maybe he'd lost his family.

The light wouldn't change.

"Have a good day," she said.

The man didn't move. He kept smiling. He watched her.

She felt for the button that closed the window. Her car hummed.

She used to listen to music in the car. She used to listen to it everywhere she could. She used to read about it and talk about it. She used to play guitar until her fingers hurt and write songs with lines like "I wanna break your home" and practice for hours and lose track of time. She used to perform her music, and weirdos cheered.

The man leaned in. From inside his nostril, a black hair hooked down. She could smell every part of him. Her heart drummed.

Something was going to happen now. Her life was going to change.

"You take care of yourself," the man said. He patted her car and limped to his spot on the grayish grass, lifting his sign high.

Behind her, cars honked. The light. Drive.

Man in the Night

I awoke suddenly in the night, as I often did, thinking I'd heard a noise, as I often did, and I rose from bed to investigate, following a dark, worn trail from bedroom to front room, where I switched on the nearest lamp to allay my fear.

In the middle of the room stood a man, flush-cheeked as if battered or buoyed by extreme weather, his grey eyes infused with the light of winter sun. If not for his strange glows, he could have strolled forth from a catalog of boring and dependable casual clothes, his hands stashed in pants pockets—though his hands weren't in pockets but black leather, so lovely in the way of certain gloves, how they hugged the hand into abstraction, a form without flaw. My bladder seized and my legs shook, but my upper half kept calm, my heart's thump, thump a distant assurance.

He smiled. For a moment, I expected him to offer his palm in introduction, but the smile soon melted into a glaze of contempt.

"Are you here to rob me," I said, "or to do something else?"

"Why would I rob you?" he said, glancing around.

"Maybe you like books?"

"Oh, I like books. But they don't do enough for me."

"What does enough for you?" If I kept asking questions, maybe we'd become friendly, have a chat. A table of hors d'oeuvres would appear and I'd excuse myself to fill a plate.

He said, "You'll see."

Yes, it was comical how I stuck my hand beneath my robe, like I'd seen resourceful thieves do in films. "I have a gun."

He laughed. "No, you don't. Even if you pulled out a revolver and pointed it at my head, you still wouldn't have a gun. You're the kind of woman who'd never own a firearm, even one in your own hand."

"How do you know?"

The flush in his face darkened. "It means I take one look at you and see everything. Who you vote for, what you ate for breakfast, what shows you watch each night. Everyone's so fucking predictable."

"That's not true. You can't tell what anyone will do." These were words I lived by. Even I couldn't tell what I would do. What was I capable of? I often fretted. Like everyone, I liked to believe that deep down I was courageous, skillful, and kind. But I also liked to believe that deep down I was craven, inept, and mean. This belief supplied me with a perverse pleasure, a confirmation of my worst fears about myself and the world, even as it fueled them.

"You can't tell what anyone will do?" he scoffed. "You *would* say that. And you would be wrong. You can tell what I'm going to do."

"What are you going to do?"

"You know. You've always known. I didn't even make it to your room. You came to me."

All the times I'd played this scenario out in my mind, everything had happened so fast, be it my escape or failure to escape. The slowness now threw me, allowed me the leisure of disbelief. Where were the instincts I thought would spring to action? Why hadn't I screamed?

"You know why you haven't screamed?" he said. "You're not scared."

It was true. My legs had stopped shaking, and I knew that was a bad sign, that somehow after all these years, I'd finally convinced myself, at the worst moment, that my fears couldn't be true.

It was hard to imagine the harm those elegant gloves could inflict on my neck. In fact, the thought of them around my throat aroused me, though I'd never been attracted to such things. What had I been attracted to? So much: Men with wry smiles and sad eyes. Women who chewed gum hard. Chatty children. Dogs: their shameless panting, their brown sugar gaze. Turquoise skies. The pure confection of new snow. The mountains, how they tore beauty into the horizon and raised the eye.

So much love for the world trapped inside my fears.

As if from afar, I commanded myself to run. I zigged and zagged like a hare, but the man blocked all ways I tried to go and what for me was graceless and sad was for him a ballet—a step here, a leap there, arms down, then wide, and when he caught me, for a moment I mistook him for a place to rest and maybe he mistook me for something else too, because we were still, I warm from effort and him warm from my life, my little, pulsing, glorious life, in his beautiful, hidden hands.

Explain Yourselves

Three years after I turned my life around and went back to college, I took an upper-level seminar. I was forty-one and the closest I'd been to being happy in a while. I'd been studying hard and keeping to myself. It worked well for me. The Literature of the American South was the smallest class I'd taken so far. I hoped it would be difficult: I wanted to take my education to the next level. On the first night, I got there early. As the other students arrived, my knee jumped up and down. I'd dressed up a little, nothing fancy, just belted slacks and a new button-down I got at Sears. I always did this on the first day of class. It was my way of showing respect. But now, in this little room, it occurred to me how out of place I must look among the rumpled sweaters and T-shirts, the old jeans, the shaggy hair. The lecture classes, with the tens or hundreds of students sitting in rows, hadn't made me feel so conspicuous.

The professor, Elizabeth Bensbirn, entered five minutes late. She wore a short, bright-green dress and white tights with giant red polka dots. The playful clothing only made her appear more pale and serious. She marched to the end of the table, dropping her books with a thud, and looked at all of us, one by one. Without a word, she passed out the course syllabus. Then she spoke.

"In recent decades," she said, "there has been much talk of men and women having different teaching styles. Men, it is said, invite competition among students, are confrontational and directive. Women, however, foster cooperation, are accommodating, and allow students more control of the classroom." She paused, again surveying our faces. "Personally," she said, "I think that's a bunch of essentialist bullshit. But since these models have some kind of currency, I will let it be known, right now, that I do not teach like a woman." She sat down. "Any questions?" she said, in a tone that invited none.

After going over the course requirements, Elizabeth Bensbirn demanded we explain ourselves. Those were her exact words. "Now it's time for you to explain yourselves," she said with a crooked grin. "Tell me why you're taking my course."

Some claimed a deep love of William Faulkner or Flannery O'Connor. Elizabeth Bensbirn nodded and smiled tightly at these responses. Perhaps she'd once had loved these writers herself, but no longer did. A couple people said they were taking the course to fulfill an English major requirement. When the second person said that, she said, "You *requirement people* are going to have to find a better reason than that to be here, or it'll show in your work."

By the time my turn came, I was nervous. I rambled. I said that I didn't know much about the literature of the American South, but I'd like to know more. I said I'd once read a Flannery O'Connor story in high school, and I didn't like it, and I wanted to see what I'd think about it now that my mind had grown. Then I said that a few years ago, I quit drinking and found God, and it seemed like the literature of the South would have something to say to both the drinker and the believer in me. There was an uncomfortable rustling in the room.

"Something to say to the drinker and believer in you," said Elizabeth Bensbirn, her smirk not unsympathetic. "I like that, Ken. Very good."

I had a feeling she liked it for the wrong reasons. Ironic ones. Still, I hadn't expected her to respond to me in any kind of positive way.

What would have happened if, when I was still married and drinking, I'd run across this woman in a bar? I saw her approaching my table, slamming her drink down like a gauntlet thrown. "In recent decades," she'd say, "there has been much talk of the different fucking styles of men and women. I do not fuck like a woman." When she'd sit down, for once, I'd have done the right thing and walked away.

At the end of class, Elizabeth Bensbirn asked if any of us were from the South. Then she said, "I'm from Alabama. But you'd never guess it."

I thought I'd talk a lot in Elizabeth Bensbirn's class, but that didn't happen. There was too much to think about. She would cut students off, say things like, "You're still stuck on the author's intent. Let's not romanticize the power of these writers' conscious minds." Or if someone would suggest that, say, Flannery O'Connor was "deconstructing class" in the South, she'd snap, "That's *not* what she was doing. Who can explain why?"

What bothered me most about Elizabeth Bensbirn is that she seemed to like me. The few times I opened my mouth, I expected her to strike me down. But she listened to what I had to say and always let me finish. "Smart question," she'd say. Or "Hmmm, provocative." I couldn't tell if I'd earned her respect or her pity.

Midway through each class session we had a break. I liked to smoke outside the Joseph Building, on the concrete porch in front of the main entrance, the Rockies at my back, where their beauty couldn't haunt me.

I prefer to stand when I smoke. The smoke seems to enter my whole body that way, not just my lungs. The other smokers in the class always found a bench together, either resting the elbow of their cigarette hand on a crossed leg, or leaning back, gazing skyward, waving their cigarette expressively. Their cigarettes looked like accessories, not, as they were for me, a substitute addiction. I found it difficult to inhale tobacco without feeling an exhilarating loss of control and wanting to brace myself against a wall.

Yet standing during smoking, during anything, always reminded me of just how much control I'd gained. In my drinking years, I'd taken more falls than I could count. The worst of them had me waking on my back in a Walmart parking lot, unaware of how I'd gotten there. My mouth throbbed: I'd lost teeth. I staggered the three miles home, through a morning breeze that stung my face, and when I got there, my then-wife, Georgie, was curled up in bed, asleep. I went to the bathroom, to see the damage in the mirror. Stretching from each corner of my mouth, across my cheeks and into my ears, was a stripe of blood. A blood smile. I didn't wash it off. Georgie wouldn't be able to ignore that. When she woke up, her face jerked back, and she looked, for the smallest moment, alarmed. Then she narrowed her eyes, shook her head, and said, to an imaginary person, "My husband looks like a clown and smells like a bitch." She got up, draping her blanket regally around her shoulders as she left the room. But Georgie didn't leave me then. That's when I would have left, if I were her.

The fifth week of class, Elizabeth Bensbirn joined me outside. She took out a new pack of Camels from her jacket pocket, thumped them against the palm of her hand, and extracted a cigarette. I held out my lighter but she motioned for me to stop and got out her own.

"I didn't know you were a smoker," I said.

She rolled her eyes. "People make so much of whether you smoke or not, as though it's some essential trait. Notice you said 'smoker,' like this single action has a whole identity attached. You didn't say, 'I didn't know you smoked.' The act of my smoking for you automatically transmuted from verb to noun. Either you're a smoker or a non-smoker. Always either/or in this culture. No shades of gray. Although I guess that's an absolute truth statement in itself. You can't win, can you?"

I took her last question to be rhetorical, though I silently answered, *no, you can't.*

"I'm sorry," I said.

She looked surprised. "What for?" she said.

"You didn't seem to like what I said about you smoking."

"Oh, no," she said. "It's fine. I just have a strong intellectual sparring reflex. Nothing to do with you."

She puffed on her cigarette, letting the smoke drift out of her mouth. She didn't smoke like an addict. All the recovering alcoholics I knew breathed their smoke in and out like a woman in labor doing her exercises to get through the pain.

"I guess I like to hear myself talk," she said. "Most professors do." She bent her leg behind her, propping it girlishly against the wall. "Sometimes I smoke," she said, "and then I smoke too much and it disgusts me and I stop. It's never become a habit, which means I get to do it whenever I want."

"That's lucky," I said.

She gave me a wry smile. "Nothing but."

We stood quietly for a bit, then she motioned to the other smokers from our class.

"Is it hard to be around all these kids?"

"No," I lied. "Not really."

"Good." She crushed her cigarette against the wall and let it drop.

After our smoking rendezvous, I studied harder than ever, finishing my other school work early so I could spend the rest of my day poring over the seminar readings, devising impressive insights. Each class, I had a little more to say, but was more careful about saying it. Before even raising my hand, I would rehearse my statement or question in my head, writing key words in the margin of my paper. When I'd finally get them down, I'd expel my words in a rush before I forgot their practiced format. At that point, I'd usually be a little behind the rest of the discussion, and when I'd finish talking, my classmates would stare at me a beat too long. Elizabeth Bensbirn, though, always seemed to come out on my side.

No matter how many times she came through, though, I braced myself for the moment when the show of sympathy wouldn't come, for a public version of the tirade she gave me about my smoking comment. Sure, she had told me that her tirade had had nothing to do with me, that it was nothing but intellectual sparring. But I wanted her responses to have something to do with me.

A couple weeks after our first smoke together, she joined me again, pulling out what I guessed to be the same Camels pack. "We're a bunch of sick fucks, aren't we?" she said, before she lit up.

"Excuse me?"

"Southerners—a bunch of sick fucks." We'd been examining attitudes toward women and African Americans in Faulkner. ("Ugh. Women and African Americans," Elizabeth Bensbirn had groaned at some poor fool. "As if they're separate categories, and black women don't exist.")

"In the eyes of God," I now said, "I guess we're all sick fucks."

"Ah, yes. And that's why He loves us, right?"

I opened my mouth, to say what, I didn't know, but she interrupted me.

"I'm not knocking God. In fact, atheists are some of the most unimaginative, soft-headed people I know. My parents were Baptists. They had a grand old time. To paraphrase Niebuhr, their lives had criticality. They believed their thoughts and actions mattered, had cosmic consequences."

I thought of my own parents: quiet, sorrowful people who

didn't expect much from life and worked hard not out of faith that they could have better, but for distraction from the fact that they could not. They were both employed at the same cardboard box factory and came home with thin white cuts on their hands. My sisters and I weren't raised with religion, though my father often blamed God when things went wrong.

But I didn't want to speak to Elizabeth Bensbirn about my personal life. So I turned to theology. "God gives our lives some cosmic dimension. But God also shows us we are puny and flawed, that our thoughts and actions and their consequences are always to some degree beyond our control and so we must rely on His grace."

"Sure," she said, staring at her cigarette's glowing tip.

"What about you?" I pushed on. "Do you think our lives have cosmic consequences?"

"I wouldn't presume to know," she said. She smiled, a little sadly, and I wanted to touch her.

"There's a kind of knowing that isn't presuming," I said, suddenly hearing the pretension in my words, which I hoped hid my desire. "Faith is always based in doubt."

She pointed the wet end of her cigarette at me. "All I do is doubt," she said. "It's exhausting."

We stood quietly, our smoke mixing with the steam of our breath in the night air, then tangling together. Had I lost her with my God talk?

"I'm not one of those God-obsessed people," I said. "I can talk about other things. I never even used to think about God until I stopped drinking."

"That seems to happen a lot. It's interesting."

"I don't know if it's interesting. It's probably not that interesting to an outsider. Recovering drunks like to talk about their drinking all the time, and how they hit bottom and picked themselves up and all that. It's an addiction in itself. I try not to."

"Why bother?" she said. "Most people *are* interested in hearing those things. They think it's romantic. Hard-living—nothing they really want for themselves, but they want the first-hand accounts so they can say they know about it, aren't sheltered. And then, the past tense, the happy ending, keeps it all from seeming *too* real. Don't you think?"

"I don't know," I said. "I've never gotten to be one of those people who only experiences hard-living through others."

"You already are, in ways you don't even realize. I am too." She crushed her cigarette and dropped it to the ground. I didn't like her telling me what kind of person I was. In protest, I put out my cigarette on the rim of the ashtray and carefully placed it inside. But Elizabeth Bensbirn was gone before she could see.

That was the last time we smoked together. I looked up her address and drove by her place a few times. Sometimes I'd catch her figure gliding across her window, as though in flight. Mostly, I saw nothing, and her tiny stucco house seemed to me like a large, smug animal, its stillness full of secrets.

In class, I found ways to respond to her questions on the spot, clearly if not eloquently, and her sharp nods renewed my confidence in her view of me. I finally got up the nerve to go to her office hours with a contrived question, to see what might happen if I once again got her alone.

When I got to her office, though, someone else was already there. I took a seat in the hallway. In front of her desk sat a huge male with hair that scraped the nape of his neck. I took out a book and began to read, but his rising voice distracted me.

"I got As in high school English. My neighbor's a senior English major, and he said my paper was really good."

"Perhaps your neighbor did not understand the assignment, because he did not create it. Perhaps your neighbor did not see the other papers handed in beside yours as bases for comparison."

"That's bogus," he said. "Teachers think they're kings. I pay good money to be here."

"Martin, I can assure you I don't think I'm a king. This is only your first paper, and if you take the time to read my comments, you might improve on your next. In the meantime, if you believe there has been an injustice, you are welcome to see the department chair."

Martin stayed seated, his back tensing.

"Martin," said Elizabeth Bensbirn.

Martin stayed put. I got up. I could see Elizabeth now, her face rigid and white, her arms crossed.

"Don't make this an incident," she said.

Martin rose slowly and stood in place, crossing his tree-stump arms.

"The first semester of college can be difficult. Most students' grades improve throughout the semester, you know. I have a list of places on campus that can help you." In her voice I heard the slightest tremor.

Martin stepped toward her and I moved in, clamping his arm.

It was surprisingly soft and easy to grip. "Time to leave," I said.

He wrenched his arm from me and raised it into a fist. My hands balled in front of me.

"Bitch," he roared into the small room as he left. She flinched, and for a second she looked like a miniature of herself, something perfect and fragile I could hold in my palm.

"It's okay, Elizabeth," I said. "He's gone."

As soon as her name emerged from my mouth, I regretted it. She returned to full size, her folded arms tightening across her chest.

"It's Professor Bensbirn," she said. "What can I do for you, Ken?"

"I had a question about the reading," I said. "But I think I figured it out." Her door clicked shut behind me.

The week after the blood smile, I'd arrived home in the early morning with a dead bird balled up in the grill of my car. I tried to scrape it off but gagged every time I got close. Georgie came outside in her robe and scraped the bird into a paper bag with a garden shovel. She put on rubber gloves and pried the remaining bloody feathers and tissue from the metal with a wet rag. "This doesn't change anything, you know," she said.

"*I'm* going to change," I said. I'd said it before. I didn't even know that I meant it. But I had meant it. I stopped drinking. And it was hard and I needed God. The thing is, God never came to me. I never filled with warmth and light and suddenly understood my place in the universe. God was a decision, like adopting a low-sodium diet. With God, I became healthy, if overly prudent. I no longer left Georgie alone every night. I stayed with her, cooked for her, helped her clean. I cut coupons from the newspaper, and if she wanted chips, I got them from the kitchen so she could stay in front of the TV. And that's when she left me—when I'd become her husband again. She'd left a note on the kitchen table: "The love's gone," it said. But that kind of love, the kind you miss, had been gone for years. I understood then that what she really yearned for was the freedom of my drinking days, a freedom I'd mistakenly thought of as just mine, and no longer craved.

The next class, Elizabeth Bensbirn seemed to display more affection for our reading, resting her hand on the open pages of *The Heart is a Lonely Hunter* as she talked. She prefaced her challenges to students with "maybe," "perhaps," or "that's a good point, but . . . ."

I raised my hand. "Some of McCullers' outcasts seem sentimentalized to me. For instance—"

"These days any sort of work that engages the affects is summarily dismissed as sentimental." She pointed at a raised hand. A girl opened her mouth to speak.

"I agree," I said. "That's not—" The look on her face stopped me.

After class, I waited for her. I asked her how she was doing.

"Fantastic," she said. "How are you?"

"You don't look well," I said.

"Yes, I do," said Elizabeth Bensbirn. She started to walk away.

What I did next was small. The smallest thing. It wasn't about sex. I don't think it was about sex.

I followed her. I touched her blonde hair.

She froze. Then she turned around, her jaw squared.

"I'm going to forget that just happened," she said. "It's obvious you're confused."

"I'm not confused. I just wanted to tell you I'm glad you're okay."

"I don't believe you."

"You don't have to," I said. "My will is good."

"Just because you believe in God doesn't mean God believes in you."

Did she know how much her words hurt? Did she care how she affected people? How she'd affected me? I needed her to know. I touched her again, her shoulder this time, and she pinched the thin skin above my wrist with her nails. "Inappropriate," she said. "Go home."

Her pinch felt good. I kept my hand where it was, let her injure me. "No!" she said, as if I were an animal, some dog.

The force of her saying it lifted her shoulder into my hand, and I squeezed. A reflex I resisted as soon as it struck. Her eyes filled with something. Fear? Pity? Hate? I released her, hurried away, before I couldn't.

Outside, the trees carved their own darkness into the night, lightening the sky. I bowed my head, put my hands together, and prayed. I prayed that if a part of me wanted to push Elizabeth Bensbirn down, press my palm against her screams, God would show no mercy.

Then I changed the prayer, and asked that He would, sending my plea into the night, where it disappeared, like a loose thread of smoke coming undone, into all the places I couldn't see.

Acknowledgments

Many thanks to the journals in which these stories first appeared, sometimes in different form: *Glimmer Train* ("Love You. Bye"); *Hobart* ("The Men I Love," published as "Willing"); *Southeast Review* ("What Family Does"); *The Normal School* ("This. This. This. Is. Love. Love. Love."); *Fourteen Hills* ("Sometimes Things Just Disappear," published as "Missing"); *PANK* ("The Speech"); *Other Voices* ("I'm Dying without You, Tom," published as "Tom"); *Five 2 One Magazine* ("How to Get Over Someone You Love in Ten Easy Steps"); *North American Review* ("Slumber Party); *Confrontation* ("Median"); *Columbia Journal* online ("Man in the Night"); *Massachusetts Review* ("Explain Yourselves," published as "Seminar).

Eternal gratitude to Amanda Miska and the Split Lip team for bringing this book into the world. And a sweeping hat tip to Jayme Cawthern for the splendid cover art!

Thank you to all my teachers, including Robert Longsworth, the late James Yaffe, Leslee Becker, Stephanie G'Schwind, Deanna Ludwin, David Milofsky, the late John Clark Pratt, Paul Trembath, and Jessica Roeder. A special thank you to Steven Schwartz: the best of this book traces back to him. Another special thank you to Emily Hammond, who is a beacon. Bonus gratitude to Steve Almond for his spectacular wisdom and kindness.

A rousing thank you to Lois Vanderkooi.

Thank you to everyone at Lighthouse Writers Workshop, especially Andrea Dupree, my teacher and dear friend, who is also The Boss (sorry, Springsteen) in all the best ways. And thank you to my students, who give me more than I can say.

Thank you to the all the writers through the years who have been helpful and kind to me in ways big and small: Katie McDougall, Danielle Akua Smith, Steven Church, Sophie Beck, Akira Yamaguchi, Susanna Donato, Laureen Harris, Dalia Rosenfeld, Dino Enrique Piacentini, Gary Schanbacher, Jenny Itell, Emily Sinclair, Kristine Langley Mahler, J. T. Hill, Michelle Ross, Kim Magowan, Michele Finn Johnson, Nicholas Grider, Tara Isabel Zambrano, Elisabeth Horan, Janice Leagra, Pat Foran, Cathy Ulrich, Katy McMahon, Dina Relles, Leonora Desar, Brad Felver, Tommy Dean, Megan Giddings, Melissa Ragsly, and many, many more. An extra dose of thanks to Meghan Barker for her supreme insight and general awesomeness, which make their mark on much of this book. And enormous gratitude to the brilliant and wonderful Erika Krouse.

Thank you to my all my friends, with a special shout-out to those who've held me up during hard times: Kim Briscoe, Travis Ritter, and Deb Briscoe; Zoë Lev; Ted Chodock; Meghan Clay Hamilton; Mary Doran; Patricia Townsend; Dianne Portilla; Theresa Stets; Anna Winkler; Dave Lindquist; Sarah Gilbert; Amy Scharff; and Norma Gutierrez Schneider.

A million thank yous to my mother, Barbara Wortman, for reading a ton to me when I was young and cheering on my writing even when it embarrasses her, and to my late father, Roy Wortman, for instilling in me a love of learning and play and independent thought. Warmest thank yous to my parents-in-law, Ann and Jim Scarboro, for their mountains of support. So many thank yous to the rest of my family, including Kara and Marc Abramson; Selma and Martin Grumbach; Marilyn Heasley and Jim Lukacs; Debbie and Harry Bernheim; Laura Bernheim; Jocelyn and Rick Hansen; Elizabeth Hansen; Arielle and Russell Weinstein; Liz Scarboro and Cullen Gerst; Catherine Scarboro and Oded Gurantz; and Jean Scarboro and Jake Beattie. And endless gratitude for the long and strong influence of those who have passed: Moses Wortman, Beatrice Wortman, Elmer Segal, and Roderick Heasley. May their memories be for a blessing.

Thank you, thank you, thank you to my husband, John Scarboro, who tirelessly supports me writing what I need to write and being who I need to be, even when it's hard. And infinite thank yous to my children, Naomi and Eli, for their sweetness and sagacity, and for putting up with me.

To properly thank everyone who needs thanking would take another book. If you've been a positive force in my life and your name isn't here, please know you're in my heart.

NOW AVAILABLE FROM

Split Lip Press

The Future is Here and Everything Must Be Destroyed
By Colette Arrand

The Quiet Part Loud
By Tyler Barton

Hungry People
By Tasha Coryell

General Motors
by Ryan Eckes

Fruit Mansion
by Sam Herschel Wein

For more info about the press and our titles, visit our website:
www.splitlippress.com

Find us on Facebook:
facebook.com/splitlippress

Follow us on Twitter:
@splitlippress

Made in the USA
Middletown, DE
04 January 2020